In Praise of Dancing at the Crossroads

"Lorna Czarnota has developed theories, stories and activities for professionals that have been used by me for several years with great success. The step by step outlines for group work in the Practitioners Guide have proven invaluable to me."

Susan McCullough, M.A., M.Ed.
National Board Certified School Counselor (U.S.)
School Counselor, Leipzig International School
Leipzig, Germany

"Lorna is a dedicated storyteller who has the gift of reaching through the barriers and touching the core of young people of all ages. Her stories present opportunities for the listener (reader) to show empathy, identify and personalize situations and look for universal truths. I have seen her touch the most resistant adolescent in crisis and provide food for thought. Lorna's stories offer a banquet for the soul."

Sylvia H. Nadler, Executive Director of Compass House
(Shelter for Runaway and Homeless Youth)
Buffalo, New York

"At-risk youth have often lived through hard times and trauma. Many of them react to probation officers, counselors, and social workers by closing up, communicating only minimally. Stories, unlike conventional helping methods, enter the brain "sideways," and youth can use stories to grapple with issues of identity and meaning. Lorna MacDonald Czarnota's skill as a master storyteller and her fifteen years of experience in working with at-risk youth have produced a valuable resource."

James Winship, MSW, Ph.D.
Professor and Chair of Social Work at the University of Wisconsin-Whitewater
Former director of Youth Services at a settlement house.

"Here in Ireland we are aware of Lorna Czarnota's excellent work with at-risk youth and their families and also in detention centers and shelters. She demonstrates how the power of storytelling can reach those young people who are most vulnerable and give them the confidence to rebuild lives which have been shattered by events which are often outside their control. Dancing at the Crossroads will prove a valuable tool for storytellers everywhere."

Liz Weir, Storyteller
Recipient of the International Storybridge Award
Cushendall, Ireland

"Whether you are a provider of emotional support to another, a person in need of guidance, or someone who just wants to understand the power of story, Lorna's thoughtful, sensitive guide won't disappoint you. Long overdue in the field of healing story, Lorna's deep research and thoughtful application of story provides what so many of us have been waiting for to guide us forward."

Lani Peterson, Psy.D.
Co-chair, Healing Story Alliance
Andover MA.

"Lorna's writings are inspirational as well as thoughtful, and full of useful approaches to the challenges of facing difficult situations and mobilizing the energies needed to achieve desired goals. Lorna's books are packed with good advice, reference material, and a true sense of humanness. Colleges and educational opportunity centers should consider Lorna's writings as guideposts for working effectively with the kind of wounded but motivated people that we encounter and serve."

Mike Seliger, PhD
Bronx Community College Dean
Executive Committee Healing Story Alliance.

"The stories, methods and ideas Lorna Czarnota has compiled in Dancing at the Crossroads will help parents of adolescents learn to communicate with, accept and mentor them through the difficult teens years."

Lynn Kratz Ryan, Parent of three
Grand Island, New York

"It is Lorna's caring heart that defines her work and her life. In her storytelling, writing, and workshop facilitating, her heart speaks in ways that encourage us to live, love, and learn, always with open minds and open hearts. She is an award-winning, degreed professional who allows neither accolades nor academe to interfere with the very delicate work of empowering people, especially at-risk teens."

Karima Amin, Storyteller, Author, Activist
Buffalo, New York.

"This body of work by Lorna Czarnota, compiled over fifteen years in practice using story to reach at-risk youth, is a long time coming and will prove invaluable to caregivers, practitioners and storytellers. Lorna includes everything that might be needed to work one-on-one or with groups of youth, and has taken great care to focus on compassion and understanding in her work with this population."

Allison M. Cox, MA Counseling Psychology
Graduate Certificate in Public Health
co-editor and contributor to the Healing Heart books.
State of Washington

Dancing at the Crossroads

Other Books by Lorna MacDonald Czarnota

Medieval Tales that Kids Can Read and Tell
Legends, Lore and Secrets of Western New York
Wicked Niagara: the Sinister Side of the Niagara Frontier Breadline Blue
Dancing at the Crossroads: Stories and Activities for At-Risk Youth Programming
Dancing at the Crossroads: A Guide for Caregivers in At-Risk Youth Programming
American and Pioneer Sites of Upstate New York: Westward Trails From Albany to Buffalo

Audio Recordings

Crossroads: Stories of Choice and Empowerment
Dancing in Dark Waters

Dancing at the Crossroads

A Guide for Practitioners in At-Risk Youth Programming

Lorna MacDonald Czarnota

with collaborations by Diana Koch

Parkhurst Brothers Publishers

MARION • MICHIGAN

www.parkhurstbrothers.com

Parkhurst Brothers books are distributed to the trade through the Chicago Distribution Center, and may be ordered through Ingram Book Company, Baker & Taylor, Follett Library Resources and other book industry wholesalers. To order from Chicago Distribution Center, phone 1-800-621-2736 or send a fax to 800-621-8476. Copies of this and other Parkhurst Brothers Inc., Publishers titles are available to organizations and corporations for purchase in quantity by contacting Special Sales Department at our home office location, listed on our web site. Manuscript submission guidelines for this publishing company are available at our web site.

Printed in the United States of America

First Edition, 2014
2018 2017 2016 2015 2014 10 9 8 7 6 5 4 3 2 1

ISBN: Trade Paperback 9781624910159

Cataloging in Publication Data will be available on the publisher's website

Edited, Cover and Page Design by: MyLinda Butterworth
Acquired for Parkhurst Brothers Inc., Publishers by: Ted Parkhurst

This book is printed on archival-quality paper that meets requirements of the American National Standard for Information Sciences, Permanence of Paper, Printed Library Materials, ANSI Z39.48-1984.

To the Healing Story Alliance
Keep up the great work you do.

Acknowledgments

Thank you to the many people who helped with and supported this work.

To my publisher Ted Parkhurst for bringing this important work to fruition and to editor and book-designer MyLinda Butterworth for her attention to detail.

Diana Koch, for collaborating on the clinical portions of this project, and for her constant friendship, support, and mentorship.

Sylvia Nadler of Compass House, Mark O'Brien, formerly of Hopevale Incorporated, and Sister Janet of TRY house. Your work with at-risk youth inspired me and what I have learned from you is priceless.

Dan Keding for consenting the use of his original the *Two Warriors.*

Laura Simms for graciously offering her version of *The Black Prince.*

To the early readers who gave feedback on my programs, you are so important to this work. Susan McCullough, Lani Peterson, Maya Opavska, and Karima Amin.

My loving life partner, Thomas Heim, without whose support I could not even do my work, and my niece Charisse, who taught me how to love unconditionally.

My parents, David and Mary MacDonald whose love of children inspired me, and who taught me about the world. You are missed more than you could know. I know you would have been proud to hold this book in your hands.

Content

Foreword

This is some of the most rewarding and challenging work of my life. When I began work with runaway and homeless teens, I had no idea what it would be like. I had butterflies in my stomach each visit for the first couple years. Some situations still cause those flutters, but I have gained enough confidence in the work and the power of story to allow myself to relax about it. I see myself as the messenger or vessel for the stories and let the stories do the real work. Trusting the stories is one of the most important things I can do in this work.

I have worked with teens that have beaten their grandmothers or later murdered other teens, which is one of the saddest parts of this work. There have been those who were pregnant, on their way to detention centers, or abused by the adults in their lives. I have not always known who they were and, in truth did not want to know. The stories find the listeners who need them, and it is important not to be prejudiced by a particular behavior or personal fear. I need to feel at ease so the youth feel at ease.

When we go to work with these young people wc must always be aware that their wellbeing comes first. Our goal is to help them help themselves. Healing often takes place in subtle, quiet ways and sometimes not until long after we are gone. We must trust the story to do its work. Every effort must be made to create a safe, comfortable, accepting environment for this work to be successful.

For those facilitators who may not have previous experience with at-risk youth, some understanding of the population is essential.

LMC

Preface

This Dancing at the Crossroads book contains theories developed and used with at-risk youth since 1994, along with workshops and session curriculums for both therapeutic youth centers and academic settings. This book is designed for storytellers, therapists, counselors, ministers, teachers and other practitioners working in various communities with at-risk youth. For stories and activities, see Dancing at the Crossroads: Stories and Activities for At-Risk Youth Programs and for caregiving advice see *Dancing at the Crossroads: A Guide for Caregivers in At-Risk Youth Programming.*

Guidance provided in this book should be modified according to the youth, facility, and ability of the presenter.

Every effort has been made to credit sources.

Therapist and social worker Diana Koch, has collaborated with me on portions of this book, and her comments and observations are noted.

Introduction

How does story heal? How does it help at-risk youth? Why is story as a healing tool so popular today?

While story is gaining popularity as a healing tool, the power of story to heal is something ancients understood. Bards, Sheneachies, and Shamans were trained to use story in sacred rituals that healed individuals and whole communities. The storyteller of the middle ages was said to be able to make or break a king with the stories they told about that person. Words held meaning and power. They were spoken with purpose.

Healing through story takes place on three levels: psychological, physical, and emotional. Today's holistic healer believes in a triad of wellbeing that includes the mind (neuro stimulus), body (chemical stimulus), and spirit (faith and belief). The physical healing that might come from listening to a story is in reaction to a balanced being. The brain releases chemicals into the body in response to certain stimuli that affect the body. Good health always has a positive influence on the spirit. Audiences hearing a story have emotional responses that trigger the release of these body chemicals. Additionally, healing stories have layers of meaning that create different responses for different people.

Healing stories can be used in many ways with at-risk youth. Crossroads facilitators tell both fictitious and personal stories as appropriate. Goals vary from modeling behavior and consequence to giving youth a voice, and creating positive adult-youth partnerships. Sometimes the goal is to afford a peaceful moment in a troubled life of a teen. All of these are important and valid uses of healing stories.

Many Crossroads programs are designed with sessions building on each other to help youth tell their story by the end of the program. Youth participants tell their stories in a variety of ways that are comfortable for them: verbally, written, poetic, musical, or through artwork. In cases where these young people have experienced trauma, this may be the first time they have told their difficult story. For troubled teens, a deep connection is made when stories are told to them as well. It is just the teen and the teller. No one else exists for that space in time. All doubts, troubles, and fears are forgotten. Things happen to characters, but the listener is safe.

Teen girls at a youth treatment facility wrote the following examples during "My Story/My Poem" sessions. The curriculum for this program is found later in this book.

Untitled
by Legs

The person your [sic] listening to now is not the same person you listened to yesterday, and tomorrow I won't be the same person your listening to today. Every day I grow a little wiser and a little more beautiful, and as a child of God every day my spirit becomes more humble and more harmonized. Every day of my life there is a lesson to be learned, a new soul to love, and an old situation to pass. Every second, every minute, and every hour counts. I believe that I am here on earth for a reason.

I give love and I am loved, and some day I hope to marry a man who needs love. I will make a difference in someone's life before I die. When I do, my body will turn into the earth, and my soul will live in heaven.

Make your life count. Cherish the minutes you live, for they are precious, one of a kind, rare and as beautiful as a diamond. Listen to your soul . . . It never lies.

Written by Sammy Lynn

I have been here for nine months. On the 13th of September it will be 10 months that I've been here. I sometimes hate it, but then I realize they are only trying to help me. I still don't have a home, and every night I pray out loud and in my writing that someone would want me. That someone would just realize all the pain I go through. I just want a home somewhere I belong, somewhere where I can live forever. I just want to be adopted. But, some people say I'm too old to get adopted and that people only want a younger child. I'm turning fifteen soon. I would like to share my 15th birthday in a place where people love me.

Love Always,
Sammy Lynn

P.S. I wish with all the world that I could live with my baby sister and that I still had my child who would have been my pride and joy. Someone who I could love unconditionally. Someone who loved me like that too. Even if they were still a baby. I think that is why I keep trying to get pregnant, and I think if I still lived with the Nelson's I would have gotten pregnant by my nineteen year-old boyfriend. If he could just hear these words I'm saying. I love him. More than anyone in the world except God. I even love him more than my real mother. I don't know if I could ever forgive my mother for giving me and my sister away to the State of New York. She doesn't know how much pain I've been going through since I was twelve.

I've been up for adoption for almost three years and not a single person has ever asked about adopting me. I feel so hopeless and useless. I would like everyone to please pray for me and that someone will come forward and say they want me.

An at-risk audience can have the same characteristics as any audience, but when working with this population it is good to know what sets it apart from everyone else. Not all teens are the same and there are developmental and behavioral variances in age and socioeconomic background that influence each. Successful negotiation relies on our consideration of each teen as an individual, but planning for effective programs requires generalization. We should also remember that not all teens have serious behavior problems, broken homes, or poor attitudes. Regardless, the teen years are "crossroads years" no matter what the teen's lifestyle or individual situation. All must cross a threshold into adulthood, even though their methods and levels of success will vary.

Runway and homeless youth are transient. Working with them in settings that may be temporary requires a different way of viewing that work. School settings, treatment centers, and some other community programs allow continued contact with the same youth for an extended period of time, whereas shelter visitations with transient youth afford us only a one-shot opportunity to influence one young person. We may be working with two or three teens, or twelve to fifteen youth of different ages at the same time. All these must be taken into consideration before we begin our planning and, even then, we must remain flexible. To do this work, we must be willing and able to enter a foreign environment and sometimes walk in the darkness. The world of at-risk youth can be a fun, playful and rewarding place to be, but it can also be unforgiving.

We cannot always prepare for all events that might occur within a session so we need to remain flexible in our approaches. It is not always possible to know the specifics of a transient teen's life and, even if we work with a group for a period of time, we may not be privy to confidential information.

We can easily open emotional floodgates or leave a session feeling as if nothing significant happened. Trusting the story and support from agency staff is essential. Someone directly connected with the youth on a daily basis, from the youth's team of caregivers, can follow up if anything needs additional attention beyond the storyteller's expertise.

We are also wise to remember than many of the youth considered at-risk have come from trauma, whether it is physical or emotional. For this reason, working with children at-risk is a roller coaster ride, requiring patience and understanding. We need to engage them in a way that is manageable and has meaning. These young people hope we will keep them safe.

1. The Abuser: Their experience with adult caregivers may have been less than positive, with their caregivers being the abusers or bystanders who did not help them. These bystanders are equal to the abuser in the eyes of these children. These children may have a sense of being sacrificed for their mothers' needs or a sense of unworthiness. Lack of trust becomes a major issue that makes forming relationships with other adults difficult.

   As healers we need to look beyond the youths' behaviors and ask how those behaviors serve them? Perhaps it helps them form a sense of internal power out of learned helplessness.
2. Learned Helplessness: The experiences of these youth teach them that only bad things will happen. Repeated incidences of trauma teach them that they cannot affect an outcome. These are the children who will create bad things so they do not have to wait for the inevitable. They leave us before we can leave them, which is empowering. They are the adolescents who may be nasty to us as a test of our fidelity. They wonder if we will hurt them in response. They will invalidate us to see if we will then invalidate them.
3. Decision Making: Many at-risk youth come from trauma and have problems making decisions because they do not think their decisions have any substance. They engage in high-risk behavior. They do not try to learn, engage in individual therapy, or storytelling because they do not believe anything can change. They have a shortened sense of future or believe they have no

future. The future will be about pain, a form of death for them.

4. Internalizing how people see and relate to us from the time we are babies develops self-esteem. Research shows that a chemical reaction happens when a baby talks, holds, and looks at the mother. When we do not have that, it affects our sense of being valuable.

   There was a little girl in a poetry group who did not feel she could write and could not read. When asked why she liked the poetry group, she said "I like the way the words feel on my ears." The experience was nurturing for her.

5. Self-Soothing and Safety: These children will internalize sensory events and self-sooth through validation and connection with good caregiving. Children who have been traumatized have not learned skills for self-soothing.

   In the book *Risking Connection* by Karen W. Saakvitne there is a story about a little girl and her father who are walking down the street holding hands. The girl is terrified and cries when a huge dog comes up barking and growling. Her father kneels down at eye level and says, "I know you're afraid because that dog scared you, but you're safe. I'm here and I will take care of you. It's okay. We'll go to the park." The child starts to relax.

   We hope children have thousands of moments with compassionate, understanding caregivers, because they internalize really important lessons about self-soothing. They learn it is okay to have those feelings. Children can and do learn to trust their feelings through experience and by the way adult caregivers react. The father soothing his daughter taught her to discern when it is safe again. Many traumatized children may never feel safe again. They may not know what is meant when we say safe or safety.

6. All adolescents, regardless of their background or experiences, want to be seen, heard, and feel individualized unless in a peer group. Trauma has core impacts that differentiate "normal" youth from "at-risk" youth. These are issues of safety and trust, especially when caregivers caused the trauma. Innocence is lost. We must tolerate erratic patterns in order to engage with at-risk youth. They come closer, go away, or come so close we cannot breathe. These children have experienced abandonment, attachment disorders, and sometimes both.

Whatever problems a young person might face or throw our way, we cannot take it personally. We must also be prepared for trauma triggers and skewed perceptions of how the world works.

Diana Koch

The lasting effect of story is something not easily measured. It's difficult even with pre and post tests. We can't see a scab form over the wound, and yet we need to know, whether for our own piece of mind, or to satisfy grant requirements, that the work has succeeded at some level.

A successful session is one that meets our intended goals. We may have both long-and short-term goals. For instance, we might choose stories based on particular issues. If a youth responds to the story with questions or comments about those issues, the story met its goal. We may also meet a youth two weeks later who mentions the story. Then we know the session was successful in reaching one young person. On the other hand, we may never know who was touched by the tale, just as teachers seldom know how they affect their students on an interpersonal and inspirational level.

We need goals. They help us focus our attention. We must also accept that we cannot always measure the success of those goals in a tangible way. It is part and parcel with the work we do. The only way to determine if a session has failed to reach its goal is to be aware of the reactions of the youth. Even a sleeping youth may be listening and this behavior may be serving them.

One of the most significant moments in my career as a storyteller came when a seventeen-year-old girl who was new at the shelter said "Storyteller, tell me a story I can hold. I want a story for someone who needs a story." She was talking about herself. My story choice did not matter. What counted was that I was willing to sit and tell a story for her alone. I then knew the session was successful for her.

In many cases, the only measure of our success may be anecdotal. Brain science tells us that changes occur within the brain that even affect physical wellbeing. Storytelling creates a trance-like state. Just as with trance and hypnosis, which have been used for centuries in healing, listeners may have both emotional and physical responses to stories.

The Search Institute developed a listing of developmental responses they call "The 40 Developmental Assets" which they believe youth should possess for the best transition into adulthood. Storytellers can use questionnaires and personal surveys as measurement tools, an example of which is included in Appendix IV.

THE ETHICS OF HEALING WITH STORY. We must be aware and make sure we know our place as storytellers. We must present ourselves honestly as storytellers, not therapists, unless we also hold license as therapists. We can tell a story we consider valuable and powerful, but we cannot heal anyone.

Listeners may find something in a story, yet it is always their choice of whether or not to use it.

We are storytellers whose stories have the power to heal, not healers who use stories. Our voices may be soothing and our appearances friendly and inviting, but the power does not reside in us. This is why we have to separate ourselves from the stories and not use the stage as our own soapbox or focus on our own healing agendas. If we can tell a good story or speak well, we can influence others. Always question whether our influences are positive or negative. Will we get in the way of our story or let the story do its job?

"The client knows when a story is told for their benefit or as a diversion from the painfulness of their own story," says Diana Koch. "So much of a survivor's trauma is relational or interpersonal that they might begin to feel responsible to the therapist or storyteller. They do not have enough sense of self and separateness to set good boundaries. Therefore, we need to maintain distance. The story needs to be a vehicle for connection and directed outward, not to the therapist's needs. A storyteller needs to create safety, knowing how to pace and time their approach to the listener. We need to know the listener's capabilities. This allows the storyteller or therapist to see and hear the client's response, to gauge how far to go."

Chapter 1

How Storytelling Works for Healing At-Risk Youth

Role of the Storyteller: Gift-Giver When listeners are ready to hear a story, they challenge the teller to entertain them. They also expect the teller to take care of them. Not all listeners will be aware of these two expectations, but they exist. Listeners entrust the teller of the tale to take them safely into the realm of story and bring them safely home again.

If a storyteller tells a story to convey his or her own agenda, the storyteller should state this up front so the audience knows why they are hearing the story told as it is. It can be helpful to use a framework question or statement for focus. On the other hand, the teller can tell a story simply because they believe it has relevance. The storyteller allows the listener to take from it what they need.

Sometimes stories teach a moral or relate to an issue the listeners have in common. However, we should not use the storytelling stage for our own healing, anymore than a therapist would use client time for his own therapy. This is not serving the listener. It is very likely that tellers are drawn to stories that speak to their own needs. This is not wrong or unusual. Believing a story can heal the teller means it can also heal the listener. However, teller healing and audience healing need to be completely separate. We cannot give the gift of story when we need to keep part of it for ourselves. Stories told for healing or entertainment, if thought of as a gift, will have no strings or expectations attached. These stories are most powerfully received because they are honest and the storyteller is "real."

Once we have taken the listeners to the edge, we need to bring them back. Only tellers who are in control of their own emotions can remain present throughout the telling experience. That presence keeps the teller and the listener grounded in the real world.

The Role of the Therapist and Storyteller

1. As therapists and storytellers who want to use story for healing we should remember this is not the end all and be all in therapy. Healing is a whole package and includes a safe environment, presentation, and knowing the audience. There needs to be a separation of roles for the storyteller or the therapist at any given time. As storytellers, we must remain present because story becomes healing when the teller notices what happens to the listener as they hear the story. A storyteller always remains grounded and aware of the listener's responses. We need to be aware of potential problems, comments, and actions from the listener.
2. Both teller and therapist must risk connection to the listener in order for the listener to risk going to the hard places. We need to risk allowing ourselves to be present with that person and every part of who they are. This will have an impact on us. Avoiding taking the client to scary places is natural in therapy, because we are afraid to go there. Good supervision is key and both the storyteller and the therapist need someone they can go to for debriefing.
3. Client behavior can get in the way, and we need to be able to filter through it long enough for them to see that we connect with the light in them. Once this happens, the listener will open and come to us. In doing this however, we risk not seeing the struggle in that person. Therefore we need to have a foot in both places, know the light, but address the darkness. The

client needs the therapist to be able to move between both, honoring the light and teaching the skills.

4. We also have to remember that the goal is for children to leave us. That loss is from day one. Our job is to help them function on their own.
5. We wear many different hats and remain separate from each piece as observer, assessor, rater, organizer, and follow-up person.
6. This work will change us and we need to be honest and acknowledge that. We must be vulnerable and healthy enough to seek help for processing. If we do not do this, we cannot be present with our work. The outcome will decline, not because the teen is disengaged, but because they are reflecting the feelings of the caregiver.

   When we step into the darkness and then back into the light, a piece of the darkness stays in our pocket. Therapist Bonnie Collins says "When you walk through a swamp long enough, you will have to shower off your legs."
7. Working in a group with a co-facilitator as a casual observer is another consideration. Co-Facilitators need to be able to take specific roles. Group leaders must be open to processing as a cohesive team. They need to talk about the hard issues that arise. The leaders should establish a "bottom line" of what they will or will not accept from each other.

   Diana Koch

In one example, a girl told the story of being gang-raped. Unfortunately, no one from the agency was there to hear her story. Unless the storyteller is a licensed therapist or counselor, the storyteller acting as outside consultant is not responsible for follow up on these issues. You must notify a supervisor.

Diana Koch reminds us that the storyteller needs the co-facilitating therapist to be in observation mode, therapy mode, and discriminatory mode. The therapist would know how far to take the client or whether to allow a process to continue. In addition, they would know when to confront behaviors in a therapeutic, nonjudgmental, or invalidating way. The by-standing therapist can do this without stopping the process and shutting off the listening.

Sometimes youth can be immature, needy, and diversionary. The helper/observer can sit near those children.

"Group" is a common term in the therapy community and can lead to the misconception and defiance. Youth say, "They are going to fix us now." On the other hand "Storytime" has a babyish connotation. We can call it anything we want, but it is our approach to it that counts. If we come to this storytelling therapy time as a place of potential, we create a community for sharing with other people who "get it."

As far as behavior getting in the way, we need to remember there is purpose in all behaviors and honor that.

Chapter 2
Understanding How Story Heals

METAPHOR

WHERE DOES THE REAL POWER OF STORY RESIDE? What truly affects the listener?

The healing mechanism in story is found in its metaphors, character events, commonality of subject, and in the trance that takes place during story listening. Caregivers can reach youth without intimidating them by speaking through the metaphors and character actions in story. Teaching them to use metaphors to tell their own stories also creates a safe environment for them to explore their emotions.

The use of metaphor as a healing device is most commonly associated with works by psychologists like Carl Jung or folklorists such as Joseph Campbell. We can find meaning in metaphors and symbols, using simple logic and our knowledge of the common symbols in many stories. For instance, children often wander into the woods and meet strangers who give them advice. Sometimes these strangers are disguised. They might really be royal or divine beings wearing a poor man's clothing, witches, or monsters. They are either kind or frightening, and have wisdom to offer which is always helpful. One simple technique for developing a healing story is to ask questions about these symbols, archetypes, and metaphors.

Examples of the types of questions are; "Why does the event take place where it does?" "Why do some characters come in disguise?", and "Why are some witches gentle and others harsh?" Mindfulness of these underlying themes can impact a listener when we tell a story. Power to heal comes from the listeners' internalization of these meanings. In fact, metaphors mean different things to different people. This is why moralizing a story weakens its impact. A story has more lasting impact if the storyteller finds personal meaning and establishes that as a focal point from which to tell the story. Allow the audience to discover the secrets for themselves. Most likely, a listener will discover it at the same time a story character is enlightened. This becomes real for them.

This book includes a basic list of metaphors and archetypes with suggestions for their meanings, however each person must decide what is significant to them. See Appendix I for a list of archetypes. Additional information on developing a healing story with metaphors is found in Unlocking the Power of Story.

"We should not be overly concerned about telling difficult stories to at-risk youth," says Diana Koch. "We should remember that 'story-killing' is not a literal physical death, but a metaphor for ridding oneself of something negative. We can temper these story moments from a nonjudgmental role. Seeing adolescents as competent individuals goes a long way toward building successful relationships."

Many at-risk youth carry a sense of unworthiness and deficiency. They are hypersensitive to those feelings. We need to create a respectful atmosphere and let them know we are in this event together. The therapist or storyteller should always create safety before entering dark places.

"In a safe environment we can tolerate and engage in hard things, because we experience 'sense-making' with attached wisdom. Include time for discussion after a story to check in and make sure the listener knows they can find help later if needed. Providing experience while maintaining distance is key. The listener can choose how close or far they wish to get," says Koch.

CHARACTER EVENTS

Character actions, and the outcomes of those actions, model life experiences. Listeners can test the situations, causes, effects, and consequences for actions from a safe distance. A story is a laboratory where the listener watches as the storyteller pours life into a beaker. The mixture will either blend successfully or explode in the character's face, but it never damages the bystander who is protected behind a shatterproof window. Once the experiment is finished, the bystanders can take or leave it as they choose. Often the listener finds the truth in the story as they "watch" it unfold for the character. Sometimes engaged listeners will instruct the character by calling out advice during a story. They already know the dangers or rewards that await the character and want to help them. We can learn about moral values and personal ethics as we observe audience response to the story and use that information for follow-up discussion starters.

COMMONALITY OF SUBJECT

What often appeals most to listeners is what the story has in common with their own situations. Writers do write best what they know, and listeners learn best from the common ground they share with the story's characters. Commonality may be physical, such as when children enjoy stories where the characters are of a similar age or slightly older. This allows children to fantasize about their futures in that same situation. It also encompasses the listener's view of self. For instance, women often enjoy stories about strong and determined female heroes. While some characters can be almost superhuman, sometimes they need to be just like us. Therefore, many heroes have flaws.

How we decide to use these stories will be determined by the focal point of the story. We must ask ourselves several questions. Is it a story about the "little guy" succeeding? Is the goal for the listener to believe they can succeed too, or is this a story where the hero is really a metaphor for the human spirit? Metaphor breaks down the complexity of human emotion into digestible bits. Whichever characteristic the story includes, the listener will feel most connected with characters who have something in common with them, their dreams, and their desires.

FINDING THE FOCAL POINT IN A STORY will help the presenter determine its appropriateness for various audiences. There are two general kinds of stories to consider when working with at-risk youth or healing story, the ones we know and ones we want to learn. We will also have known audiences and unknown ones. In other words, all stories can be used but require different techniques for understanding, and we will not always be able to select stories for a specific audience.

If we know our audience, we can have the luxury of choosing the focal point that fits their needs. How this is done may depend on whether we are telling a story already in our repertoire or learning a new one. If we do not know the audience, but wish to add a story to our repertoire, we should develop the focal point around that which drew us to the tale in the first place.

Stories are often multi-layered and can fit many situations depending on what we decide to accentuate. The following will help us craft our stories according to audience need.

UNLOCKING THE POWER OF STORY

Unlocking the power of story is a method designed to help storytellers find the heart of the story. Using this method they can determine where the story's power is found, develop, and craft the story for telling without losing its impact.

When using stories for therapy and healing, we need to know why a story influences us, draws us to it, and feels powerful. Understanding the use of metaphor can help us become better crafters of story and help us impart this power to our listeners. As the crafters of tales we must first come to terms with the story and discover its heart for ourselves. Although we do this, our audiences will ultimately find their own meanings and power within the stories we tell, which is our primary goal.

Finding Story Power. To find the power of story, we need to let go of the story, allowing it to be separate from our individual emotional attachments. We can use any number of methods to achieve this goal: look at a story's perspective, discover why we like or dislike a tale, or explore the storyteller as gift-giver. We can breathe new life into the story through visualization or using the Goldilocks Method, found on the following pages.

Story Perspective. Learn to see the tale from a different point of view by telling the story in first, second, or third-person, or look at the motivations and responses of different characters in the story. Take on their roles as tellers and become empathetic to their lives, ideas, and needs. Doing this helps us gain new insights about the story and ourselves. Even those characters we think of as villains have something to offer. Try introducing an outside character and allow that character to tell the tale, placing us in a neutral position very much like that of the narrator. Perspective is one part of the process of letting go and does not necessarily need to be placed in any particular order with the additional methods that follow. In fact, some methods will happen simultaneously. The more we experiment by changing perspectives, the more we will learn about the story and strengthen its impact. Let the listeners choose sides when they hear the story, something they will encounter in real life.

Discovering Why We Like or Dislike a Tale. It is said within the story-telling community, "We do not find the story, the story finds us." We could take immediate ownership of these stories or allow ourselves time to stand back and investigate them before deciding to utilize them in any particular way. By postponing our immediate reactions, we will be more likely to break our emotional ties to the story. It is also quite possible that the actual power or heart of a story is in what we find fascinating or appalling in a tale.

Sit with the story for a while before deciding if it is the right story for you or for your listener. One way to do this is to ask what bothers us about the story or what attracts our attention. If there is something that troubles us ask why is it in the story. Is it a classic detail found in other stories or unique to this tale? Is it typical of the culture from which the story comes? The more out of place the detail appears, the more likely it is to be empowering in some way and it deserves closer scrutiny. We should ask the same question if the detail attracts us, especially if it is a traditional detail. One example is the number three. Ask, "Why are there three and will the story be different if I change that aspect of it?" Never change a story without exploring these questions.

While our modern culture has many ideologies contrary to what many folk stories teach, such as the stepmother being wicked or the witch being destructive, these are classic archetypes. We need to understand them before we delete or change these details. Deleting details from a story simply because our culture does not accept the ideas can be damaging to the power of the story which ultimately speaks to our primal selves.

Archetypes and symbols should not be taken literally. They are representative. A witch is not necessarily a follower of Satan who puts spells on people out of evil intent, nor is the stepmother simply to be considered a father's second or third wife. If we think of these archetypes in that way, we will most likely consider them negative role models but they hold meanings that lay deeper beneath the surface of the human psyche. Archetype examples can be found in Appendix I.

A fellow storyteller once asked my opinion of a detail in a story she was learning. It was a Chinese story about a painter whose painting came to life. His paint was mixed with the "spit of old men." The storyteller felt a little uncomfortable using this detail in the story; she felt that it was not pleasant for her audience. She asked my opinion. After some research of Chinese culture and magic, I found that a major ingredient in creating a magic potion was sometimes spittle. Because the Chinese venerate their elders, the spit of old men would be very potent. Without this ingredient, the painter's works could not have come to life.

Another example is the witch in Hansel and Gretel. It may seem cruel for Gretel to push her into the oven to destroy her, but not doing so takes away the children's power over what kept them enslaved. One might change the witch's destruction to another means such as having her run away but a witch on the run is still a danger to the children in the story and children who come along later. Having the children shoot her instead of burning her also changes the power. Shooting is in fact more violent because there is no potential for the witch's wisdom to reincarnate. The witch represents wisdom, not evil, and by burning her we allow her and her wisdom to rise again, just as the phoenix rises from the ashes. Our world needs that wisdom to be reborn again.

There are versions of Little Red Riding Hood where the girl shoots the wolf instead of being captured and escaping as older versions suggest. Listening to these stories is fun, but the story loses its healing impact when the girl so easily defeats the wolf. If she shoots the wolf, the girl has no opportunity for maturing from an adolescent who uses force to gain her needs, to become a woman who uses wisdom to overcome adversity. The wolf archetype is male but in general terms he represents a go-between, a catalyst to move the girl into womanhood.

Though we live in a society that empowers women, changing old stories to fit our new ideas may not allow the power of the story to shine. The fact that these stories are as popular today as centuries ago should clue the storyteller to their power. While we can use the story to meet our own agendas, we limit their use and miss the other possibilities. Letting a story go requires us to accept it at face value, allowing its inherent power to find the listener. Storytellers need to question what they should or should not change, without bias of their own beliefs. To do this effectively, consider the needs of the audience first.

For example, for telling to at-risk audiences, Crossroads modified the ending of the story "Mary Culhane and the Deadman." In the traditional tale, Mary digs up the gold revealed by the Deadman and becomes wealthy and lives happily ever after. Since many at-risk youth will "sell out" for a quick dollar on the streets, the adaptation in this book has Mary drop the shovel and not take the gold when she realizes her soul is at risk. This sends a much stronger and more relevant message to the at-risk teen audience. Another viewpoint on having Mary take the gold would be to consider the gold to be a metaphor for wisdom gained. Story money isn't always real money but to make this point the teller should use a framework statement or question.

Breathing New Life into the Story. When the storyteller/story crafter is separated from the story they wish to tell, tearing the tale apart makes it easier to work without prejudice. Finding the power of story requires analysis toward the goal of reworking the story, which should not be confused with rewriting or changing the story. It is more like midwifery with the teller bringing the tale into the world.

It helps to find another storyteller or objective friend who will not judge the telling of the tale. They can listen to it and act as the storyteller's mirror. The storyteller tells the tale and the listening partner answers back, "What stood out as interesting? What was troublesome? What seemed strange or appalling? Where in the story was there a powerful image?" Using this method to release a story helps the teller "see it through a listener's ears." These new insights strengthen our ability to tell powerful stories.

To make the most of the storyteller's time and effort, look for stories that serve many functions, addressing a myriad of issues. These multipurpose stories are the ones most worth adding to the repertoire. Also consider creating several different rituals and activities to go with each story and a variety of situations where they might be told. These stories and activities will be a strong foundation for most of the healing storyteller's work.

Visualization for Unlocking the Tale. The storyteller's ego, expectations, voice, and appearance have an impact on the power of story, but the story must be able to stand-alone without these distractions in order to heal others. Using a guided visualization to develop a strong story will separate the storyteller's ego from the tale lending more objectivity. Try using the following visualization on a new story. Have pen and paper ready for note taking.

Imagine a space completely void of color and texture.

You are neither in nor out of this space. The absence of color and texture creates a space that is black with no light present. Now place a closed box inside the blackened area. Within this box is the story you wish to tell, but you have not seen the setting, the characters, or plot of this tale. It is unknown to you. A crack forms in a ceiling above you and light from an unknown source seeps slowly in, filling the space.

Simultaneously, the box opens. The walls of a room now come into focus. They are covered with the contents of the box. The floor and ceiling too become part of the story's setting.

Take note of the first five things you see. What are they? Do they represent anything in particular or are they just incidental details? What, if anything, is their significance to you and to the story? Jot this information on your paper but don't think too much about it right now.

The scene now becomes three-dimensional with objects and characters from the story. See their specific colors, textures, emotions, and movements. Is anything significant? Does something seem out of place? Does one thing stand out more than the others?

When the entire box is empty, the room is filled, and you have a good picture in your head of the most prominent setting, characters, and the plot, open your eyes and begin writing your thoughts.

Do not edit, just free-write. The goal at this time is not to write the story itself. Write a simple list of what was sensed about the story's power and heart. These thoughts can be either specific or general.

Tell your partner the story then share any thoughts about the visualization. Now share any insights and retell the story from this new perspective. The words used may or may not be the same as before the visualization, but new meanings will have been discovered. This process can affect voice, posture, and speaking rhythm. Coming from this fresh insight gives the story new impact.

DISCOVERING GOLDILOCKS

The Goldilocks Method allows the storyteller to analyze a story according to its archetypes and symbols. The teller first lists all the symbols in the story. Assign meaning to these symbols and choose the most significant ones. Then, tell the story in first person. The final creation does not need to follow this first-person telling, but by using that point of view, the storyteller will gain insight about the story. If the story was originally told in first person, the teller should choose a non-central character's point of view. This new character can be any of the characters, narrator, or even an inanimate object, such as the broken chair.

Using this method brings storytellers to a better understanding of their stories and story choices. This groundwork will strengthen the story, while still allowing listeners to find their own meaning. It is also possible that the listeners, especially teens, will not find power in a story until something happens later in life that causes them to recall what they heard. A truly powerful story is like a token carried in the pocket. Our hand touches it and reminds us it is there. We may never use it, but it may come to our aid at a time we least expect. When we realize this we begin to approach story not only for entertainment, but also as an instrument for teaching and healing. Not only does this enhance our stories as storytellers but it also increases the impact of story on personal development.

Several instances in my life led me to a deeper understanding of the power of story and ritual. One such instance was when I discovered I was Goldilocks. That was a day that changed the way I approached story.

I was working for the Midway Caravan, a wonderful program developed for teaching children about the circus and themselves through imagination and active participation. I was the "Teddy Bear Lady." My job was to engage children in the act of make-believe by encouraging them to help me create teddy bear stew and tell stories. I was to include at least one bear story. The only bear story I knew was "Goldilocks and the Three Bears."

The Midway Caravan was contracted to run their program at the CNE, Canadian National Exhibition, which was a huge fair held each summer in Toronto, Canada. We were there for ten days and my schedule ran from opening, at ten in the morning, until approximately six in the evening. I had a lunch break and about one additional hour off during the children's circus time. The rest of the day was spent engaging the children in play anytime a child showed up. That meant continuous work or just sitting and waiting. It made for long days and hard work in a hot summer environment.

I always began with a make-believe activity and then told a story or two, including Goldilocks. When I asked what the children thought the story meant, they replied, "Don't go into someone's house when they're not home" or "Be careful of strangers." While these are important lessons for young children, after about three days of telling Goldilocks, I had enough! I was not going to make it another seven days with this.

I thought to myself, Goldilocks is a stupid story. Then again, it has been around for so long. There must be something to it, but what? It needed to mean more to me or I knew I could no longer tell it.

The story needed a fresh approach. Maybe I would tell it in the first person, as if I were Goldilocks. But first, I was going to have to know her better. Who was this girl? Why did she have golden hair and blue eyes? What was she doing wandering in a forest alone? Why did she walk into someone's house when they were not home? And, who were these bears? Why did Goldilocks run away instead of befriending them? None of it made sense to me and I needed answers. Where was I going to find those answers? I got them from Goldilocks herself, of course.

Taking Goldi back to my motel room that evening, I made her lie on the coach. I said "So Goldi, tell me about yourself."

I'm not sure exactly how it came to me, but I decided the answers were buried in the story itself. They were hidden in its metaphors. I sensed that the metaphors most likely remained constant to the tale even over centuries of retellings, so that is where I began. I listed all the symbols in the story and assigned each a meaning. My list included all the colors, numbers, and symbols such as the list that follows.

girl (innocence)
golden hair (light, purity)
blue eyes (sky, open to adventure)
forest (the unknown)
house (security)
knocked (politeness, seeking entry)
nobody answered (refusal of entry)
entered (need to enter, perhaps by force)
kitchen (comfort)
table with porridge (nourishment)
three (classic number)
too cold (non evasive)
too hot (evasive)
just right (personal and self-empowering, satisfactory)
ate it all (devouring of the wisdom of self-knowledge)
living room (a place of community)
chairs (relaxation)
too hard (no comforting)
too soft (overly comforting, stifling)
just right (perfection)
broken (realization of false comfort)
stairs (path leading up or down)
ascend (moving to the next level, upward, forward)
beds (a chance to rest)

too big (not restful, expansive and overwhelming)
too little (stifling and small)
just right (perfect)
fell asleep (too perfect, allowing for settlement)
bears come home (true ownership)
wake her up (an awakening, motivation)
girl runs away (continues the journey)

This was a time of transformation and transition for me. I was divorced and had just changed careers from fifteen years as an interior designer to graduate student looking for a teaching position. I was passionate about becoming a teacher and also had a huge student loan to pay off.

Meanwhile, I had been telling stories for a few years and the art had gotten "under my skin." I had been utilizing stories in substitute teaching and as a student teacher. I found story a powerful way to reach children especially those with special needs.

Complicating my decisions was the fact that my father had helped me pay off my student loan after I persuaded him that I should be a teacher, but now storytelling had a strong pull. I never realized the power of that pull or how anxious I had been feeling about the decision until that night with Goldilocks. I had a calling and Goldilocks was my epiphany.

I returned to the fair the next day ready to tell Goldilocks in a new way, in first-person.

The story began, "Let me tell you about something that happened to me when I was a little girl."

Throughout the story, I never mentioned Goldilocks by name, yet the children knew the story. When I finished, a little curly haired girl in the first row looked up at me with wide-open eyes and said, "Y-y-you're Goldilocks."

That moment changed my life.

I replied, "You know, you're right. I am Goldilocks."

I knew then that I was that little golden haired innocent girl looking for what was just right for me. I had gone on "the great adventure." Wandering through the unknown, I came to the secure place. When I knocked, nobody answered. They could not, because that place was for me alone. I entered and found a table filled with things to try. My parents had nourished me, but only one was just right for me. Entering the adult community, I tried what my father and mother thought best and what was supposed to be right for me, but it was not. The situation broke down like the story-chair broke down. I ascended to the next level of my life. I took comfort in what was on that new level and almost permanently fell asleep in that place of comfort. Thank goodness the bears came home and woke me up. If they had not, I would never have continued my journey. I will never fall asleep again. I have listened to my intuition and learned to see the hidden truth. I have become more accepting of changes in my path. My career and the way I looked at stories changed and Goldilocks led the way.

Framing a Story. Telling a story with a framing statement or question strengthens its therapeutic benefits and gives the listeners a purpose and focus, without detracting from their ability to take what they need from the story.

With a grief group we might begin a session by saying, "We have all experienced the loss of someone we love and respect." In this way, a truthful statement has been made without passing judgment on the thought process or telling the listeners what to think. Placing these statements or questions before, after or within the story can add impact.

The following is an example of how a guiding statement might be used inside the story. When the children, in Hansel and Gretel, find the pearls and gems in the witch's cottage, as stated in the Brother's Grimm version of the story, we may easily assume they are literal gems and pearls. But in the Crossroads retelling of this story, the storyteller might add "In the corner they found gems and pearls—the gems of wisdom and pearls of knowledge." This avoids supporting the idea that wealth is a solution to our problems. Calling the treasure wisdom and knowledge supports the idea that rewards are not always monetary. Showing the solutions in story context holds more weight for listeners than any lecture on morals and ideologies.

Use restraint when changing or adding to a story. The power of the spoken word should not be overlooked for its potential to be helpful or harmful.

Remaining detached from our individual ideals and needs when telling a story to at-risk youth is imperative, as shown in the section on The Ethics of Healing Story.

It is not necessary to frame a story by making a statement, but doing so aids with segueing into follow-up activities and highlights significant issues. For instance, in the story of Vassalisa, a doll given to her by her mother represents the mother's wisdom and guidance. It also represents the intuition that can be found in us all if we learn to look for it. This can be the framework for the story, "All the knowledge and wisdom we gather from the people around us and our experiences can be used to help us on life's journey."

A storyteller might also share personal experiences about listening to intuition and finding an answer or inspiration in their own life journey. Before telling your story simply state, "We all have these little voices, but it takes time to learn to listen to them." To reinforce this story, use an activity such as creating a small doll for Vassalisa.

Personal Myth for Identity Development. Comfort comes to the listener when identifying with or dissociating from the characters in a story. At-risk youth find relief in commonality with a character and reassurance that they are better off than some.

It is the listeners' ability to discover their own myth that makes a story useful for healing. Exposing adolescents to as many stories as possible provides them with role models and a better understanding of themselves. Once listeners take on the "truths" of a character archetype, they subconsciously begin testing their choices. They think about what that character would do in a given situation and what consequences would exist for those actions. Any story character can be broken down into a variety of archetypal characteristics that have something in common with most listeners. Story becomes a testing ground for life.

For instance, classical heroes have specific abilities. They have courage to face the unknown and naivete to look past the dangers. Unknown to them in the beginning of the story, they are not alone in the quest; a guide or helper shows up unexpectedly. Heroes also often have super powers or magic items. These aspects are vital to the hero and part of his or her entire self.

These are all symbolic of average things found in everyday life, but camouflaged by characters' larger-than-life depiction. They must be grandiose to encompass complex varieties of the human experience. The characters' abilities must be noticeable.

When working with at-risk youth, the storyteller has the added responsibility of helping the listener discover these everyday meanings within the story. Specific story heroes will have unique or accentuated characteristics. For example, Hercules has physical strength whereas, Sir Gawain of Arthurian legend is endowed with youthful innocence.

Young people may be better equipped to make thoughtful choices if they connect with one of these characters. The healing power of the story is in the storyteller's ability to accentuate or highlight these powerful story events.

Story Structure as a Telling Guide. Ritual and formula are the structures in story that mimic life. Stories have a beginning, middle, and an end. Characters do not just appear in the story without some kind of introduction. This is true in life and we as humans are used to this repeated pattern. Listeners need something to set the mood and carry the character into the story. The middle of a story will include a climatic event or turning point in which change affects the main character and the end of a story may be quite definitive or phrased so we know it continues beyond the story we have heard, for example "They lived happily ever after."

It is important to note that this phrase does not tell us what happened to the characters after the story, but does tell us that whatever the trials faced during life, that character survived happily. This is a very powerful message for at-risk youth. The closure in story is necessary for the listener to feel satisfied and a story needs to lead us somewhere or at least beg us to imagine the end of the tale. Some definitive ending is necessary, even if the ending is not happy. This might be one reason why we seem to want to hear the teller say, "They lived happily ever after" or "Snip, snap, snout. This tale's told out" or "That as they say is that." The listener wants to know the storytelling is on the same journey and the journey has been completed.

Some people have become dissatisfied with "formula" stories and try to interrupt the natural sequence of story to create something fresh. These "fresh" approaches to well-loved, time-tested tales can fall flat. As listeners, we are conditioned to expect and anticipate certain outcomes and many times these are tied closely with our desires to find love, success, and meaning in our own lives.

The movie the "Princess Bride" is a wonderful example of this. The grandfather in the story visits his sick grandson and reads him an adventure story. Throughout the movie, the grandfather teases his grandson because he is reluctant to have his grandfather read to him. His grandfather attempts putting the book aside or twists the story structure. The grandson objects to his grandfather leaving without finishing the tale. At one point, he tells his grandfather that the book cannot end that way. He says, "The bad guy can't win!" These basic human ideals remain fresh in the world of storytelling. They give us comfort and hope, and are soothing to youth living in turmoil.

One exception to this formulaic rule is with the personal story, which does not represent an entire lifetime but only displays one moment in an individual's life. By itself, the personal event might have a definitive ending, but the person's life continues beyond that event and if they are still alive, that story is still being written. The personal story can be a very powerful mechanism for reaching at-risk youth for this very reason. The stories of their lives are not finished and they still have control over the endings. This becomes a tool to explore cause and effect and consequence for action.

When working with at-risk teens telling their life stories, we only see a glimpse of an event, not their whole life. These life stories are works in progress and are often troubling to them as well as to us. Helping the teens finish these stories is important. Remind them that these events are only chapters in their life story, not the end of it. Their life stories have many possible endings depending on the choices they make. The events in anyone's life drive the story forward and determine direction to some extent but the writer, the person living it, has full control over the next sentence, chapter, and direction the story will take. To help youth work on their lives we need to teach them something of story structure and help them explore possibilities. This is one of the major goals of education.

One technique to help youth flesh out their personal stories and to give them safe distance to explore those events is to have the teens frame their stories in a folk tale or fairy tale format. Instead of "I", ask the teens to use "he", "she", or "they". Two interesting things happen when the teens format their stories in this way. They are given the ability to complete the story with a favorable ending and are able to see their stories at a distance as it happens to someone else. If problems reside in a youth's family, they can even create test families and work through a variety of scenarios.

Without the prejudice we bring to our own stories, the answers become clearer. We view our story with more compassion, empathy, and impartial judgment, as we might with someone else's dilemma. Letting go of the story allows the story to develop a life of its own and resolutions present themselves more readily.

Even when using this process, we must find a way to close the chapter and create an ending to this part of the life-story. One way to do this is to add a statement or aside as narrator of the tale. For instance, the storyteller might say, "And I hope they find their way," or "I hope they make the right choice." Giving voice to these hopes helps make them real. This is also true in ritual ceremony. One must speak one's intent. It is important to remember not to tell the listener what to think. Our statements just give focus on an issue and solidify a closure.

Story structure acts as a guide for the storyteller. For example, a storyteller just learning a story may have difficulty deciding where or how to begin the tale. Using a traditional structure such as "Once upon a time," helps move the story forward. It triggers the correct words we wish to say, even if spoken silently. This story starter also sets the storytelling moment apart from the rest of the day and signals participants to listen. This is also a great technique when participant clients have difficulty starting their stories.

Chapter 3
Designing Sessions

Once we know our stories and how to use them with our intended audience, we are ready to learn about the agencies we are working with and how to structure a program for them. Beginning storytellers and anyone new to this kind of healing work will need to spend more time learning stories than those who have been telling longer in these settings, but even experienced storytellers will find it necessary to continue researching stories for their work. However, there are ways to utilize and enrich repertoires more effectively. The following tips also assist practitioners with at-risk youth program development.

1. List the types of issues to be addressed. A suggested list of common issues is found in Appendix III: Youth Issues and Story List.

   View your existing repertoire and other stories to see what will fit those issues.

2. Using that list of stories, you can plan for smaller sessions dealing with specific issues. Also, see "Discovering Goldilocks" for another approach to developing healing stories.

3. When preparing for one or more sessions, start with an issue or theme in mind for the overall program such as making choices, finding mentors, creating legacy etc. Explore the details in your stories and select a method for delivery whether you wish to use framing statements and questions, use poetry, song, tell the stories in one session or over many etc. Create activities for the selected stories.

If you use these steps consistently you will eventually have a set of stories and session designs you can interchange as needed and you will feel prepared, which incidentally will make you more comfortable with the at-risk population. Just remember to remain flexible also.

Many unknowns exist when working with at-risk populations that can cause anxiety for the presenter. Concrete designs give the presenter comfort; preparedness helps alleviate stage fright. Awareness is empowering and helps us become deliberate in our actions giving us some control of our environment. Structuring of a presentation increases the impact, eases anxiety, and acts as an outline or container for the session. However, for all our planning, we should not become rigid. Flexibility is essential when working with adolescents because regardless of our plan, we will not have control of all factors and this population will put us to the test.

The storyteller should consider collaborative partners, such as staff or therapists working for the facility where programs will take place. If the storyteller is running sessions outside an agency, he or she may still want to have a therapeutic partner. Also consider involving the youth as part of the planning process. These collaborators and partners supply extra support and additional viewpoints.

Collaborating with Agency Staff. Anytime two people come together for some purpose, there are bound to be differences in ideas and ideologies. All partners should know their function within that purpose. This is especially true when a storyteller comes from outside an agency to deliver services. Several things need to happen for a successful partnership.

First, if the storyteller is not a therapist, he/she should consider having an agency representative present at all times during sessions. This covers the storyteller if something happens that requires immediate intervention, while allowing the storyteller to remain in the role of teller rather than disciplinarian. Having an official agency staff person present also covers the storyteller from liabilities. Agency staff should function as casual observers of the youths' behaviors in case issues arise that need addressing by therapeutic staff. Always remember, safety first for you and the youth.

While the storyteller may set rules and boundaries for the group, it is best to make sure agency or house rules are incorporated. If teens are not allowed to fall asleep during sessions, this may need to be a group rule as well. Always discuss any differences in opinion and theory with the agency before making changes.

The purpose of these separate roles is to keep the storyteller in the role of gift-giver and mentor as much as possible. This helps build trust and respect; youth will remain more open and honest with their feelings. If the storyteller must take on the role of disciplinarian, they may not be able to maintain that sincerity and the young people will shut down.

Rules for Group Behavior. What may be acceptable behavior in a classroom, home, or among typical teens, may be quite different in a therapeutic setting. The outside storyteller may anticipate loud talk, uncooperative attitudes, foul language, violent and eruptive behavior, name-calling, over activeness, or sleeping youth. Many of these behaviors are part of the disorders at-risk youth experience. Each storyteller must decide what is considered acceptable within the boundaries of the agency rules and his or her own level of comfort.

It is typical for teens to test the newcomer before deciding to accept them. Keeping this in mind will help the storyteller get past the most difficult early meetings. It often takes up to four sessions before the majority of teens will begin to cooperate with the group leader and possibly longer before they will cooperate with each other. Sometimes they never reach a point of mutual respect.

Very basic rules should be in place in every group with the understanding that agency staff will reinforce them when necessary. The outside storyteller needs to stay out of the way of agency staff. None of the following rules will be followed during the first session in most settings. It is wise not to expect them to be followed to perfection at all times, but to use them as guidelines for eventual outcomes.

Respect for the speaker. This rule covers anyone who is talking. Youth and adults are expected to listen. Active listening is something that must be learned over time. You may consider this successful with some low-voice talking, as long as the youth or adult who is talking is not drowned out by others. Do not expect the teens to be completely silent. This talking-out behavior can be to your benefit. So many teens spend the day in classrooms or settings where talking is stifled. As soon as they have an opportunity, they will become boisterous and giving them a voice is what you are trying to achieve. But lack of respect should not be tolerated.

How we deal with youth not following the rules is as important as setting them in the first place. Getting into lengthy discussions about misbehaviors or pointing out that they are not following the rule, will only lead to more interruption. Make sure you're not spending as much or more time talking about not talking than actually telling them a story or involving them in the activities.

In this situation, it is best for the group leader or storyteller to remain silent until noise subsides or change up the work to a more intense level such as using a story that is strange and demands their attention.

If a youth participant is the designated speaker, instruct him or her to remain quiet until everyone is ready to listen. The group leader may need to change activities, tell a story, or use a change of voice, such as singing to bring the session back to order. It may be necessary to split large groups into smaller ones or end a session if talking-out behaviors continue. Group dynamics change dramatically in this way.

Always keep a calm voice and demeanor, using hand signals whenever possible. Do not further agitate the situation by appearing frustrated, fearful, or insulted.

Name calling is not allowed. If youth persist in insulting each other or the storyteller, get physical or disruptive beyond control, the session must end. Staff people will intervene.

IMPORTANT: Sometimes at-risk teens just want storytellers to prove their worth. They are so used to abandonment that they may actually expect the group leader to leave and not return. Returning for the next session after an outburst goes along way towards building trust and respect. Never point out the bad behaviors at the next session. What's done is done. It would be better to discuss or review positive behavior rules.

Moving about or sleeping. Learning styles differ. Sometimes youth need to move about in order to focus, others need to sit on chairs, the floor, or close their eyes. If a teen falls asleep, assume they need it and be assured that something gets in the cracks of their subconscious.

For many at-risk youth, falling asleep may be a strong signal that they have come to a place of such great trust that they know they can sleep without being assaulted. Some may need the sleep mentally and emotionally. This could also be obstinate behavior, or sleep could be a warning sign of greater problems such as drugs and alcohol, or even a side effect of medications.

There are many factors at work in these behaviors. The outside storyteller will get to know their groups well enough over a couple sessions to determine which of these messages sleeping youth are sending. Agencies and staff may have preexisting rules about sleeping during group.

The storyteller will be best served if they ask the staff to do the intervening, but may have to reinforce this alone. If the storyteller must ask a sleeping youth to remain awake during sessions, it is best to use voice variation, proximity to sleeping youth, or vary the level of activity to keep them awake and focused, rather than interrupting the flow of material to tell them to wake up.

Remember, when setting group rules it is best to keep them simple. Use rules that might already be in place within the agency and let the agency be "the bad guy" whenever possible. In some situations you can involve the youth in creating the group rules.

Group Number and Age of Participants. The actual ages of group participants will be determined by the agency where the youth are located. Basic storytelling models apply if the storyteller has a choice regarding which ages will be placed together. Most at-risk youth agencies have children between the age of twelve and eighteen. It would make the most sense to put the younger teens in groups separate from the older ones if possible. Just be flexible if you must have mixed ability and ages in a group.

Keep groups small in number whenever possible. Between six to eight participants is a good number for interaction without as much disruption. Groups of twelve may work in some cases. Groups of two to three may be necessary, but will not allow for as much interaction and variety of ideas.

Expect dynamics to change if group size changes. Sometimes it is necessary to have a large group for some work, but split into smaller groups for other activities. Each situation requires different formats with the goal for the youth participants to have the best experience you can offer in a safe environment.

Teens are almost adults and must learn to function in a world of variety so keep group size, age, and activity as close to real life as possible. Remember, preparation for living as contributing adults is the ultimate goal. Each group will function according to their particular needs and must be individually assessed. This is also true of individual group members.

Have a standard plan, but be flexible. Keep in mind the audience and what is available as repertoire. Each situation will require some planning depending on your knowledge of the audience and issues with which they are dealing.

Predetermined Audience and the Existing Repertoire. If you know your audience in advance, for instance all sixteen-year-old boys with learning disabilities, begin with what you know about working with that population. Decide what their most significant need might be.

Also consider venue. When working in a school setting, ask the teachers what they think the teens need to get from the session. This becomes the session goal. In a shelter or detention center setting, ask about overriding issues that the teens are dealing with at this time. There may be many issues at hand but choose one on which to focus. If the needs are extremely varied try focusing on generic ideas such as hope, loss, the future, or choices. Choice and consequence are major topics for anyone in need of empowerment.

Next consider your existing repertoire and look for metaphors, symbols, or characters that meet the chosen issues and goal. It may be necessary to delve deeper into each story, bending them to fit, but most stories have multiple layers. Keep in mind, bending a story does not mean changing it. It means adapting the story to tell in a new way. For example, the story of Rumpelstiltskin may look like a simple fairy tale about a queen who tricks her opponent. She is clever in overcoming him, but to a mother who is fighting for custody of her child this story is very significant. Rumplestiltskin is a life or death battle for that young mother and many at-risk adolescent mothers are in situations where they must achieve success to regain their children. If the storyteller knows this, the story takes on a new meaning for them and their listeners.

A storyteller should be careful when changing stories that have been in existence for a long time. These tales have already survived the test of time because they speak to the human condition. However, subtle changes can be made while maintaining the initial impact of these tales. See the section on Unlocking the Power of Story.

Look beyond any preconceived notions of who should hear a story. Approach the tale with the audience in mind by asking what they might see in it. By doing this, we may discover that a character in the story that we originally found insignificant is a significant archetype and role model. This newly discovered character might become a driving force, as in the story of Vassalisa. In this Russian folktale, the doll is important to her journey's success and is just as central as the main character or the witch. In addition, the setting of a story or the characters' words may change to fit the listener's experience, while the story structure and elements remain the same.

We may use stories we already know or learn new ones for a known audience. The major difference in adding a new story from using an existing one is in the amount of research required.

We should search for several versions of the story before deciding which one to tell. It is also possible, using the methods outlines in Unlocking the Power of Story section, to meld several elements of each version to form a new one. When reading variants, it is common to find things included in one version and not the other. Before deciding which details to use, ask why they are there or why they were excluded. Sometimes, exclusions and inclusions are a product of culture, religion, and the era or viewpoint in which the story was told. Victorian society cleaned many old stories to make them socially acceptable, as has the Disney® Corporation. Cinderella by Brothers Grimm is not the same story as Disney's version. Our ideas regarding stepparents and other family structures continue to change.

When restructuring a story, never remove a detail before considering why it was there in the first place. The following is a sample session for a well-known children's fairytale that surprisingly speaks loud and clear to at-risk teens.

Chapter 4

Hansel and Gretel Sample Session

The following is an example of how to build a session around this story, which can be found in *Dancing at the Crossroads: A Guide for Caregivers in At-Risk Youth Programming*. Additional sample sessions are found with the stories in this book.

Sessions should include a framework question or statement, story, follow-up activity, project, and/or series of questions. Follow-up questions can be answered verbally, in writing, through an art project, or they can be food-for-thought. They can also be used as jumping off points for stories written by the youth.

Using art and role-playing for expression is less threatening for at-risk youth who have learned not to trust their feelings to others. They can "hide" behind the art; making it an effective way for them to tell stories. See page 135 for information on mask making.

The following is an example of a framing statement for the story of Hansel and Gretel and may be used before or after the story is told. "Life is a journey and we sometimes hear stories about the hero's journey. This story could be one of those." By using this statement we have invited the listener to wonder why we said this about this story. That causes them to focus on that statement while listening or before beginning an artwork.

Keep these framing statements and questions simple and open-ended. Inclusion of a song or poetry as framework for story adds dimension to a session. For example, one might begin Hansel and Gretel with the spiritual, "Motherless Child." After telling the story, allow the teens to write their own verses to sing together. List their ideas on chart paper.

Encouraging the teens to create their own lyrics, models bonding through common experiences. The following is an example of a song written for this purpose. The youth may laugh at the adult singer, but it should not be taken as an insult. While children hear teachers and caregivers sing to them, teens are not used to this experience which can make them temporarily uneasy. Laughter is just their way of expressing this discomfort. Once the adult presenter and the youth gain trust, singing together can be a fulfilling bond. Furthermore by showing vulnerability, the adult takes a step toward building respect born of courage, which alternately helps the youth find courage to overcome their self-consciousness. It is another opportunity to be "real" for them. The teens will appreciate validation of their feelings and take comfort in knowing that someone else shares these experiences. When we share things we have in common with others we find safety and this is most obviously modeled when working in groups rather than one on one.

Never discount the power of vulnerability. "This is the gift of healing," says Diana Koch, "when the youth finally has the space to hold the feelings and have them honored and witnessed by someone else. A step in healing is to honor the skills you have learned through the act of survival."

The acquired strength, power, motivation, or knowledge from a traumatic experience can be called the "gift of trauma." Survivors often discover the ability to effect change through healing. For instance, many victims' rights organizations have been formed following personal traumas, including "Mothers Against Drunk Drivers.""

The following song sample was written by the author and later incorporated in Crossroads presentations of Hansel and Gretel.

Wind and Rain

by Lorna MacDonald Czarnota

Refrain:
Oh the wind and the rain,
Oh the heartache and pain,
Got a hole in my heart,
Oh the wind and the rain.
And I'm drowning in tears,
And my soul's bleeding out,
Want to run to the mountain and shout,
Oh the wind and the rain.

Refrain

And it's been many years,
Since I've seen the sun,
And they say you must crawl, then you walk
But I learned how to run.

Refrain

And you know not to cry,
And you learn not to care,
And you say you won't tell, which is true
Cause there's nobody there
You're all alone.

Refrain

Use the following for discussion following Hansel and Gretel.

"In many stories the witch is cruel, but witches in stories are usually keepers of wisdom. The witch in this story does help the children. How did she help them? Is there someone in your life who has taught you a lesson of some kind?"

Session leaders should share personal experiences with their groups when appropriate. An example of one personal experience, Funeral for a Friend, and its activity can be found in *Dancing at the Crossroads: A Guide for Caregivers in At-Risk Youth Programming.*

To finish the Hansel and Gretel session, give the teens a tangible reminder. The gift can be a gemstone representing wisdom or a glow-in-the-dark pebble to help them find their way. Using a tangible item from a story imbeds the message. At-risk youth like to receive gifts no matter how small. These small gestures of kindness usually surprise them because they are unaccustomed to people giving them anything without strings attached. A list of resources for gifts and materials can be found in Appendix V: Materials Resource List.

UNKNOWN AUDIENCE AND THE EXISTING REPERTOIRE. Preparing for an unknown audience requires a different approach than knowing the audience specifics. In this care, focus on an important issue, but be prepared to change directions once you are introduced to the group with whom you will be working. Have a flexible plan.

Select generic stories that reflect as close as possible the interests of the at-risk population. In some cases you may want to ask the venue director which stories will be appropriate. Choose favorite stories that previous audiences have enjoyed and make sure you choose your best and most practiced stories. While children can be forgiving, at-risk teens are not always as welcoming and you do not need to do anything to increase your anxiety. This is not a time for experimentation—do what you know best.

If you are new to this work you will eventually get to a place where you recognize your most powerful stories and the effect they have on your audiences. Use caution in the beginning because powerful stories may open floodgates you are unable to handle within the format of the program. These responses to difficult stories will require your supervisor or collaborator's attention, which is why it is advisable to work with agency staff, at least while you are learning what to expect.

Storytellers must always take care of the audience. If we know a story might cause an emotional outpour, we should remind the listeners that they may speak to us after a program or if the venue has a therapist on staff, remind the teens that they should consult with them. It is always important to remind the listeners to take care of themselves as well. If a story is difficult, in some cases, it may be necessary to allow youth to leave. However, do this only if a staff person can supervise them.

Leaving at a difficult moment in a story is not always advisable, it can cause more harm than good. If youth appear agitated at a difficult point in the story, encourage them to see what happens, to wait it out and sit with that discomfort for a little while. Most upsetting stories have good endings or at least ones most listeners can cope with hearing. Unfortunately, if a distraught listener leaves before the story is finished they may not gain necessary closure. The resolution remains incomplete. It is only upon hearing the entire story that we can learn from it.

Chapter 5
Rituals & Coming of Age Ceremonies

This chapter includes several opening and closing ideas, and activities for coming of age ceremonies; openings set the time apart as something special, closings create a sense of finality.

It is very important for youth to experience structured activities that have a framework including opening, body, and closing. Many at-risk youth have experienced just the opposite of structure in their lives. They have had no warnings, no closures, and few special moments. Structure may be unfamiliar to them, however they will appreciate it and once you establish these routines many teens will remind you if you forget them.

OPENINGS

YARNS: Use pieces of yarn to represent our stories. Each person in the circle speaks, answers the session leader's question, or tells a story while tying a piece of yarn onto the group ball of yarn. Holding the ball of yarn while speaking creates a stage for that individual to speak, much like the Native American tradition of the talking stick. The quick growth of the story ball often surprises teens. Holding onto something while talking also helps them settle and become less self-conscious about sharing. You will have to tolerate them playing with the yarn as it is something they will toss and squeeze. This activity also helps them feel like part of something larger than themselves.

SPIRIT GUIDE: Have youth close their eyes.

Note: Some at-risk youth may have trust issues and may not keep their eyes closed. It is important when building trust to allow the youth the opportunity to do things as they feel comfortable. Do not force them.

Spoken by the Session Leader: "You are a tree deep in the forest. Your roots reach down into the earth where they find the nourishment they need to make you tall and strong. Your branches stretch upwards toward the sky and the warmth of the sun. You are strong and one of many trees. Look around you. You might see the other trees standing near. You may hear sounds, perhaps running water or birds. Take a moment just to feel the earth beneath you and the sky above: To hear and see.

You now see something coming toward you. It is an animal, but you know it is a friend. It might be flying or crawling. It is a friend and has something to tell you. You can invite it to crawl on you or land on you. Listen to its voice. Hear its message. When you have heard your guide, open your eyes."

Remind the youth that their guide is a private friend and they do not have to share. This is very important in giving the youth control to withhold or share their feelings.

Ask willing youth to share their experiences and messages. Another option is to let them write it down and place it in a sealed envelope with their name on it. In this way they will remember the message and know it is safe from prying eyes.

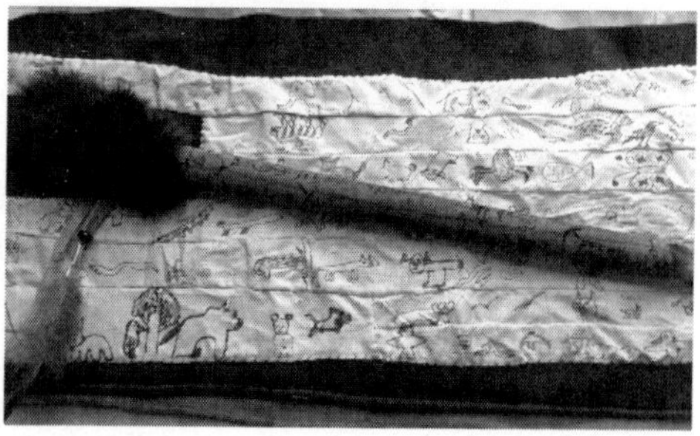

TALKING STICK: There are many forms of talking sticks. One design is to use a wooden dowel 1" in diameter covered in a material than can be drawn on, such as soft suede or other cloth. Wrap the open ends by tying the handle end with a suede tie and dangling feathers and the top end with rabbit fur or other material.

Each person in the circle holds the talking stick as they speak. This gives them permission to be the speaker and signals others to listen.

The youth may sketch their guides on the stick. Add strips of cloth or suede if more room for drawings is needed. Use a permanent marker for drawings. This does consume time.

STORY STARTERS: Depending on the situation, you may begin a story with a question or statement that will set the tone for the story, creating a focus without telling the listener how to feel about the story.

For instance if working with anger management issues ask, "Have you ever been angry about something? How do you react to those things that make you angry?" Answers from the teens are not necessary, you really just want that issue to be in the forefront of their minds as they listen to your story. If desired, allow them one answer each or just tell the youth to hold onto their thoughts until after the story. Upon completion of the tale, ask them to share some behavior they would change.

An appropriate statement for anger management issues might be "We all get angry, but everyone reacts to that anger differently. We cannot change others. We only have control over ourselves."

The following are other sample statements, questions, and visualizations for various issues. Choose an appropriate story for each issue.

LOSS of a cherished friend, relative, or mentor: "We are lucky if we have had someone in our lives who has been there for us. Sometimes we lose those people. In some cultures they believe that after a person dies we must never speak their name again. In other cultures, we encourage memories of those people. By speaking their names and telling their stories, we keep their memories alive. We honor them because they mattered. Is there someone you would like to honor?

Before we share, let's get a good picture in our heads of our loved one. Sit in a comfortable position and close your eyes. Let a picture of your loved one flow into your mind. See them. What are they wearing? What does their hair look like? Can you see their face? Is there a smell? A sound? A touch? Where are they sitting or standing? When you see them clearly, open your eyes."

Allow each youth to speak the name of their loved one and say what the relationship was with them. They can tell anything they want about that person. As with all activities similar to this one, strong emotions can surface and we should not force anyone to participate who is not comfortable doing so. As with all healing work, make sure they know they have staff support.

As each young person finishes his or her story, the group says the name of that loved one in unison. It is a way of honoring the lost person and the one who loved them. Many at-risk youth may also want forgiveness from a lost loved one.

Losses of other kinds include a job, a home, or a possession. Use a similar sharing circle for these.

For example, if a job is lost have the participants picture themselves at work and ask them to share what they liked or disliked about it. Discuss what they would like to find to replace their loss.

CHOICE: "We make choices every second of every day. Choosing not to choose is a form of choice. Sometimes we make choices that do not go well for us. Have you ever made a choice like that? If you could make one wish to change the outcome of that choice, what would it be?"

Answers can be given verbally or you may tell "Star Woman's Basket" and use the follow-up activity[1] suggested for that story.

KEYS TO THE DOOR: Opening a door is a very symbolic idea. Finding interesting looking keys at yard sales or antique stores is easy. Some craft stores sell tiny key trinkets in the beading department.

Have the participants close their eyes. "Envision a door. Something very important is waiting behind that door. It is a gift for you. It is a place you would like to be or a thing you want to have. You are not really sure what it is or how it looks until you unlock the door."

Place the key in the youth's hand, and ask them to unlock the door and see clearly what is behind it. Have them open their eyes and examine the key. If they are willing, ask them to share what they find.

Visualizations of this type are intentionally short due to the attention spans of this population. They can be expanded for groups that can handle longer sessions.

[1]The activity for "Star Woman's Basket" can be found on page 138 of *Dancing at the Crossroads: Stories and Activities for At-Risk Youth Programs.*

CLOSINGS

CLOSING CIRCLE: The following is an example of a closing circle.

The teens stand with their left palm up and right palm down, covering the palm of the person on either side, but not touching. This idea of "not" touching is an important recognition of individual space and privacy. However, touching has been shown to have a healing quality, so we lightly touch palms at the end of our circle. Everyone in turn will say their name and pass energy or good thoughts to the person on their right. These thoughts are unspoken. When everyone in the circle has spoken their name, we gently press that "energy" into the palm of our circle partners. Then we squeeze hands. The group leader can make some kind of wish for everyone depending on the issues covered. For example, if you have been dealing with grief, wish for them to find peace in their hearts. When dealing with relationships, wish for everyone to love self and come to the place of love they want in their lives.

The act of figuring out which hand faces up or down is a process leading to presence, it breaks the spell of story and brings us back to the real world, grounding the listeners in the here and now.

STORY ACTIVITY: Before closing the session with a circle, wrap up the individual stories. Giving young people something tangible is a good way to help them retain the images and messages from a story. This might be an artifact from the story such as a grain of rice for the story "Grain of Rice.[2]" It could be the creation of a craft piece, such as a mask.

For example, when working with anger management issues, ask the youth to write their anger on a piece of paper and burn it. They can also make a medallion of hope from Fimo clay (see Appendix V: Materials Resource List).

Wish boxes are also fun. These can be made using cardboard jewelry gift boxes, breath mint tins, or non-dairy creamer containers. The teens place objects, words, magazine pictures, or anything of significance to them in the wish box. Craft sticks with written affirmations can be substituted for objects when using non-dairy creamer containers.

Let the youth decorate the outsides of these containers. Always be sure to give a few extra sticks to each youth so they can add to their wish box later.

[2]"Grain of Rice" story is found on page found on page 62 of *Dancing at the Crossroads: Stories and Activities for At-Risk Youth Programs.*

When finished with the activity, the youth may share their creations. While this should not be forced, encourage sharing for making their wishes more real.

RITES OF PASSAGE

Char's Thirteen Stones: This activity is based on the story of Sleeping Beauty. It was the tradition in her kingdom that the godmothers of a child gave the baby wishes for successful living. Each of Beauty's godmothers gave her a wish. They were beauty, wit, grace, song, dance, and music. Grace, beauty, and wit are good for this ceremony. Additional wishes might include safety, security, love, intelligence, humor, empathy, strength, health, courage, and creativity.

Use any number of stones and wishes, but thirteen is a classic number and the first teen year. Gemstones can be purchased in large wholesale quanti¬ties at a reasonable cost. See Appendix V: Materials Resource List.

Assign a wish to each stone and write it on a sheet of paper. Place the stones and the paper in a decorative bag or wrap each stone in the wish.

Explain to the teens that they are about to receive some very important wishes for their lives from someone who cares about them. Tell them about the story of Sleeping Beauty, although this is not necessary. If the youth is from your immediate family or the child of a friend, suggest they prepare by showering or bathing before the ceremony. This is symbolic of shedding the old before accepting the new. The teens should dress in their favorite cloths just as they would for any special occasion. Supportive adult mentors are invited to attend the gift-giving. Food following any ceremony is always a fun idea and adds to the fact that it is the community that promises to guide the youth. Preparation adds importance and meaning to the ceremony, placing it apart from mundane activity.

Each adult can gift one stone, or the group leader can give all. Read each wish as the youth drops the stone into the bag. Consider lighting a red candle and a white candle before the ceremony begins. The white candle represents the youth's innocence as a child. The group leader buries the candle following the ceremony. If preferred, it can be kept as a prayer candle to light when the youth needs some of their youthful innocence, such as when they encounter setbacks along their journey. The red candle represents the youth's arrival into the adult circle. Give this candle to the youth or keep it for them to light on each birthday. The candle may also be lit as they succeed throughout life.

Always check with the venue you are using for fire codes before lighting candles in a ceremony. If it is not allowed, you can light imaginary fires or use LED lights.

INITIATION INTO THE ADULT CIRCLE

Necklace Ceremony: A necklace ceremony is another ritual for marking a youth's arrival into the adult circle. This is done much in the way of the Thirteen Stone ceremony.

Invite each adult mentor to bring a bead, or the group leader can buy beads for everyone to give. The lead mentor, who may be a parent or guardian, should supply a larger bead for the necklace center.

A group leader (GL) will officiate the ceremony.

Goal: To help a teenager transition into adulthood through a heightened sense of maturity and acceptance among adult peers.

Opening: Initiate-youth sits separately, to the left or right of the adult circle. He or she is draped in a black netting or cloth representing darkness before birth. The group leader acknowledges the gender appropriate ancestors.

GL "Grandmothers (Grandfathers), welcome."

GL "Mothers (Fathers) welcome"

GL "Aunts (Uncles), daughters (sons) and all female (male) relations, welcome."

"Light candles for those who are no longer with us that the youth may wish could be present."

Each woman or man in the circle should give a reason for being invited. What can she or he bring to the circle to help the young person on her or his journey?

GL "We are here to bring a new young person into our circle. Her (his) name is (name). Who can speak of this young person's qualities?"

Someone should have prepared a few things to say about the initiate.

GL "Does (name of youth), have something to say for herself (himself)? What do you bring to this circle of adults?"

If the adults in the circle agree they bring the initiate to the center of the circle to sit.

GL "When you were born you came from a place of floating comfort and quiet into a world of light and chaos. Your first sounds were crying and you will cry often in your life, but today is a day of joy." (Slowly unwrap the netting or cloth.)

GL "The umbilical cord connected you to your birth mother. It was cut and you became a separate individual. As a child, you had to rely on the adults in your life to feed and clothe you. Today you are welcomed into the circle of adults. You are still young and need their help in a different way. They will guide you, support you, and help you with the years of their experience. Today you become a young woman (man). First, you must break the ties that bind you to your childhood."

The initiate's mother holds a silver or white cord or ribbon. The initiate holds a pair of scissors.

GL "Once this cord is cut, you cannot look back. You must look forward to the coming adventures in your life."

Initiate cuts the cord. Light a candle representing young adulthood.

GL "Let this candle stand for this day like a first day in a new life. Light it each time you make a choice that helps you on this journey as an adult."

The group leader tells a story. "Vassalisa"[3] is suggested for girls, "Sir Gawain and the Green Knight"[3] for boys.

Initiate will take her (his) place in the adult circle.

GL "We will now gift our new sister (brother), beginning and ending with her (his) closest relative."

"Vassalisa" and "Sir Gawain and the Green Knight" can be found in *Dancing at the Crossroads: Stories and Activities for At-Risk Youth Programs.*

In turn, each adult now comes forward with a gift bead and speaks of their gift to the young person. The closest relative ties the necklace around the initiate's neck.

GL "Welcome (name)."

The group leader or circle members may acknowledge any relatives not present and the new young adult may receive a new name at this time. This is fun for them but not necessary.

The new member of the adult circle blows out the candle. Wrap it in decorative cloth and place the candle in a box to keep.

Hugs all around.

GL Closing: "We thank you our grandmothers (grandfathers), mothers (fathers), sisters (brothers), aunts (uncles), and friends for attending this special day and ask your hands to guide our new member on this journey and to help her (him) make good choices. May we all to listen to wisdom and hear our ancestors' voices inside our hearts."

Blow out remaining candles.

TIME TO EAT!

Chapter 6

Crossroads Program Curriculums

The following are several curriculums designed over fifteen years for work in facilities that have time for longer programs. Most run once per week for six to eight weeks. These curriculums include outlines with materials lists and detailed instructions for running groups with boys and/or girls.

MOMMY AND ME®: A CURRICULUM FOR TEENS WITH TODDLERS

The following Crossroads Story Center program, Mommy and Me®, teaches mothers to tell stories to their children, especially personal and family stories. These mothers are sometimes homeless teens. The principles of Mommy and Me® are to allow mothers to re-visit their childhoods, create an environment to help stop abuse and illiteracy, form bonds between parent and child, and develop a sense of community and personal identity.

Many young people today know little of their genealogy and lack a sense of belonging. Mommy and Me® was created to address this problem. All children need to develop personal and community identities in order to thrive as adults with a foundation for the development of their morals and understanding societal standards within a community.

The following eight-session curriculum, designed to be two hours each, was prepared for use with homeless women and their children ages two and up. The woman ranged in age from nineteen to thirty-five. This curriculum is also appropriate for younger teen parents and their children.

The term "session leader" can be interchanged to mean whoever is telling the story during that session, whether it is the storyteller-presenter or caregiver participant.

Please note that in most cases session plans include more information than can be covered in one session. This allows the presenter to run longer sessions and also allows for freedom of choosing what to cover without as much chance of running out of things to do. It is always better to have more than less.

Presenters should keep the sessions lively and fun, remembering that many at-risk youth missed much of their own childhood and need support and some playtime, too. If it is fun for them, they will make it fun for their children.

Curriculum Outline for Mommy and Me®

Number of participants: Group Number should be restricted to no more than ten parents if possible.

Eight Sessions Overview

Sessions I-II:	Whole group sessions with children and parents. The Purpose of these initial sessions is to familiarize the participants with storytelling, the session leader, and to model positive adult/child interaction. If necessary, the group leader can limit this part of the curriculum to one session instead of two.
Sessions III-VII:	Storytelling Basics for Mom's with Young Children: Principles of Storytelling. Story content, Story length, Method of delivery, Reasons for using storytelling, Building a story repertoire for the busy mom. When to tell stories, Why Tell Stories.
Session VIII:	Sharing and Final Gathering

SESSION I: GETTING TO KNOW YOU

1. Introduce the presenter and set rules for the sessions such as how the room will be set up, how you expect participants to sit (children on the floor with or next to parents etc.)
2. Explain what to expect during the program and what the outcome should be. Give out any handouts for the sessions, as you deem appropriate.
3. Presenter tells a personal story about his or her childhood.
4. Activity: Pass the Face, No I Won't (Hamilton & Weiss, *Children Tell Stories*, 2005.) One person is it and decides on an emotion then makes the face of that emotion to the person sitting next to them, who passes it to the next person and so on until the last person tries to guess the emotion. This is a good icebreaker, usually makes people laugh and sets them at ease. It is also a good example of how stories change from one person to the next. This is something to let parents and children know, they should not judge each other's stories on accuracy but remember that each is an individual memory.
5. Invite any parents or children to share a story about their childhoods.
6. If time permits, tell some sample folktales and other stories from your repertoire appropriate to the participants.
7. Explain what will happen in the next session. Each parent and child should decide on a simple folk or fairy tale they recall from childhood or this session to retell as a team the following session.

SESSION II: CONTINUE SESSION I AND BEGIN STORY WORK

1. Team retellings.
2. Give out any necessary handouts.
3. Explain that the next few sessions are for parents only. The children will return in the later sessions to hear stories from their parents. This program was designed where daycare services were available during the next sessions. You may need to adjust accordingly

4. During each of the following parent sessions, you should introduce a new type of story and/or give parents a chance to tell some story examples. Do as much or as little of each suggestion as time will allow. The most important thing is to give the parents what they need in each session. It should never be a race to complete the curriculum.

5. Always try to give a brief overview of what will be covered at the beginning of each session, a recap at the end, and an idea of what will be covered in the consecutive session. Give out handouts as appropriate. Parent handouts may be found following this curriculum along with a bibliography of appropriate reading.

SESSION III. STORYTELLING BASICS

Story Content: Share the following ideas with parents and share a sample story for each concept, if possible.

1. Vocabulary is experiential: Yolk or Yoke, Heir or Air

   Children will only understand things in stories if they have had experiences with them in life. The storyteller may need to introduce new concepts. This can be done as an aside in the story or before telling.

2. Old story ideologies: Wicked stepmothers and missing fathers.

   Standards and beliefs have changed since the early stories were first written, but the metaphors remain consistent as in good versus evil, caring versus selfishness, finding the way in troubled times. We should always be mindful of the hidden messages in stories and how a given audience might perceive them.

3. Using Stories and Concepts

   A. Scary versus Sweet: Scary stories can teach children when to be afraid. They should be age appropriate and told with respect for the story and the listener. Adults should never tell scary stories just to see how much they can scare a child.

Suggested stories:

"Hansel and Gretel" (Brothers Grimm)

"The Ghost with One Black Eye," Priscilla Howe, *The Ghost with One Black Eye and Other Stories*

B. Morals and lessons: Children will listen to stories at times they may not be willing to listen to adults lecture. When telling stories with a lesson, explaining the moral is not always necessary. It is usually best when the lesson is shown through character and plot. Show, Don't tell.

Suggested stories:

"Being Greedy Chokes Anansi," *Favorite Folktales from Around the World*, Jane Yolan.

"Two Friends: How They Parted," *The King's Drum*, Harold Courlander.

"The Boy Who Cried Wolf" (Aesop)

C. Silly, nonsense: Sometimes stories should just be fun. Silly stories can teach language skills and new concepts such as color, shape, and numbers.

Suggestions:

Nursery Rhymes

Going on a Bear Hunt, Michael Rosen, Walker Books.

SESSION IV. CONTINUED STORYTELLING BASICS

Story Length and Venue: Older children sit longer than young children, but if disabilities are present even older children may have short attention spans. Adults will not sit long if the story is boring. The storyteller will need to engage the listener in different ways depending on their attention spans.

Pre K-K: 5-10 min per story, 20-30 min per program. Grade K by themselves can sit for forty-five minutes. Props and energetic stories can help hold a young child's attention.

Gr. 1-2: 5-20 min per story, 45-60 minute per program. The better the child grasps the story concepts, the more likely they are to listen.

Gr. 3-12: 5-20 minutes per story, 45-60 min per program.

Grade 7-adult can also sit for stories that are 30-40 minutes or longer if the story is relevant. Longer stories can also be told as a series of smaller stories on consecutive days.

Venue: A listener will sit longer if they are comfortable, the story is engaging and relevant. Sitting on the floor for a short time is possible, but anyone will get wiggly if they become uncomfortable. Young children enjoy blankets and pillows on the floor, but may be tempted to lie down or fall asleep. The teller must decide if this is appropriate. The room should not be too hot or cold and if possible, use soft lighting.

Method of delivery: Use props to help with the stories, especially for very young children. Seeing something can help make the story real. Gesture and facial expression also lend clues to meaning in a story.

1. Some props for use in storytelling include felt boards and puppets. Some children find puppets frightening. Use them with caution when working with possible abuse victims. Pedophiles sometimes use them to abuse children.
2. Additional Aids for Engaging Listeners
    - A. Repetition: especially for very young children and to elicit participation, enhances good listening skills.
    - B. Participation: Children will often join in whenever repetition is used such as a choral verse. Use simple hand gestures for the children to mimic. Sometimes using gesture can signal the audience when to participate. Teaching the parts to the audience may be necessary. This will depend on their individual abilities. Be flexible. Some listeners will join in without prompting. You might also consider teaching the participation before or during the story.
    - C. Song and Music: Breaks monotony, adds dimension and interest. Include music, such as drumming, to accent a story when participation is required.
    - D. Costume: Hats are a wonderful way to use costume without taking away from the story. The storyteller may also use full costume.

Use caution, costumes can be as frightening as puppets for some children. It is best not to use costumes or props unless they enhance a story. Do not use them without a specific reason.

E. Props should not take away from the story, but can help with comprehension. For instance, when telling the Russian folktale, "The Enormous Turnip," parents might show a turnip to the children in advance. This helps the child understand what a turnip is and acts as a springboard for after-story activities such as cooking and eating a turnip.

F. Standing versus Sitting and Audience Placement: The storyteller should be at eye level or just above the audience. If they are seated on the floor, sit in a chair. If they are seated in chairs, use a stool or stand when telling. This will help with behavior control during telling and avoid too much neck strain for the audience. Do not place listeners where they will need to look into bright lights or be distracted by views and noises.

G. People coming and going from a room is distracting, so make sure the entrance to the space is behind the audience, not behind the storyteller.

SESSION V: REASONS FOR STORYTELLING

- Enhancing listening skills
- Teaches imbedded lessons
- Builds imagination
- Strengthens comprehension of story structure
- Creates bonding with community and family
- Builds personal and community identity

BUILDING A STORY REPERTOIRE FOR THE BUSY MOM

Telling stories can be time consuming if we must first learn the stories. While it is a good idea to find and learn new stories, it is also possible to start with what we already know. Here are some suggestions to make the job easier.

1. Start with simple, short stories. Stories can be one minute to an hour in length. Most children's fairy tales are between five and ten minutes in length when telling.
2. Use familiar stories. Recall some traditional stories from your own childhood, such as "Goldilocks and the Three Bears," "Little Red Riding Hood," "The Little Red Hen," "Chicken Little," or "The Gingerbread Boy."
3. Half read/half tell. Find a child's book and read through it. Telling most of the story is possible while holding the book and reading parts of it to the child. Reading the entire book is also a good activity for a parent and child, but telling part of a story allows the parent to watch the child's face for reaction and maintain behavior control.
4. Tell familiar stories from different viewpoints. *The True Story of the 3 Little Pigs* (Scieszka, 1989) is a popular child's book. It is a very funny new twist on an old story. The parent can tell most stories in this way. For instance, if the storyteller knows the story of "Goldilocks and the Three Bears" she might tell the story as "Baby Bear Meets a Stranger." Other alternative viewpoints might include "What Happened to Mama's Cooking?" or "The Bears Come Home." That is potentially four or more stories in one!
5. Share personal experience stories. Childhood experiences are some of the most important things a parent can share with a child. Of course, these should be appropriate to the age and experience of the child, but this is what helps a child form a family and cultural identity. For example: A child might ask what mom's name is. Instead of just telling the name, tell the story of how the name was given and why. This will create a lasting memory for the child to be passed down to his or her children.

SESSION VI AND VII:

When to Tell Stories

- Bedtime
- When the child needs to be close to you (scared, sad)
- To teach a lesson
- To share a family experience
- Anytime a child wants to hear a story and is ready to listen.

Activity I: Retell a story.

The group facilitator should tell a short simple story that beginners can easily learn. Have the session participants retell the story to a partner, and then share with the whole group. Emphasize that it does not have to be perfectly polished, but they should try to tell the entire story in their own way. After this activity, the parents will have practiced one story and added a possible story to their repertoire.

Why Tell Stories

PARENT CHILD BONDING THROUGH LANGUAGE AND TOUCH. Touch and early language are important for a child's development. Several historical cases exist of children locked away and deprived of these things (*Analysis of Environmental Deprivation: Cognitive and Social Development in Romanian Orphans*, Sandra R. Kaler & B. J. Freeman, 2003). This has resulted in the children being underdeveloped for their ages, sometimes permanently so. These children have been unable to develop speech at a full adult level later in life. A window exists when our brains can soak up language, process it, and act upon the ideas creatively. Additional information on speech development is available through the American Speech-Language-Hearing Association (http://www.asha.org).

If a child misses that window, language development is stalled or halted. We can say the same of appropriate touch. When infants and young children are deprived of touch, they can become adults incapable of trust and closeness with others. They tend not to function well socially. This is so important that many hospital wards for sick infants and children now incorporate time for special volunteers and nurses to hold these babies and talk to them. Many foreign orphanages such as those reported in Russia and the Ukraine are classic examples over recent years where forgotten children suffer mentally, physically, and emotionally.

EARLY LITERACY AND IMPLICATIONS. Highlights of this session are indicated in the parent handouts that follow this curriculum. The list included below shows that between one and four years of age children have developed their language skills at a very fast rate. These skills include color and number concepts, shapes and sizes, word accumulation and sentence building, basic understanding of grammar, and some printed word recognition.

The following information is based on varied sources including *Baby Play* and *Toddler Play*. For more information on these two books see the bibliography that follows this workshop.

LANGUAGE DEVELOPMENT: Stages are approximate as not all children develop at the same rate.

- Age one: Children speak their first words, literally no understanding of hidden objects.

  Use read aloud books with repetitive rhythmic phrases such as "Patty Cake" and "Peek a Boo." Peek-a-Boo is popular at this age because children believe that what they cannot see is not there.

- Age 18 months: Children make two-word combinations using nouns, verbs, and some adjectives. They form sentences such as "baby sleep," "milk gone," "see mommy." Learning new two-word combinations is slow.

  Read aloud with simple phrases and actions. Simple hand games like "Where's the Baby," a version of Peek-a-Boo.

- Age two: There is a sudden surge of two-word combinations.Children enjoy read aloud picture books, walks in the park and hand games.

- Age three: The child may have learned as many as nine hundred words. They have added adverbs, pronouns, prepositions and adjectives. The child enjoys playing with the sounds of words, names and identifies actions in pictures, can identify large and small body parts. Adults should provide activities to stimulate language growth, picture books and nursery rhymes, and stories with action pictures.

  The child enjoys action stories in picture books, books with words identified by pictures that show colors, shapes etc. They like the word play in nursery rhymes.

- Age four: Children can make grammatically correct sentences. They begin to question why and how. A child may have fifteen hundred words. They like to play with sound and rhythm in language. Children use past tense, but not always correctly. The child might say "he goed," "the baby sleeped," and "we plays ball." The child uses language for world discovery, listens to and says rhymes and riddles, and discusses action in books with prompting from an adult. Let the child talk about what they did yesterday, read books and discuss pets, families, people, and environment. Allow children to discuss characters and actions. Explore walks in the neighborhood, zoo visits, and trips to the store together. Experience becomes an important part of learning.

  At this age, language becomes more abstract and they may increase their word bank to twenty-five hundred words. The child may understand the prepositions over, under, in, out, in front of, and behind. They enjoy reading or listening to stories with more complex plots. The child can retell stories or make up their own from pictures. Introduce the use of concept books and practice asking and answering questions. Read books explaining why and how.

- Age 5-6: Children acquire words faster and may have as many as six thousand. They understand complex sentences, and use correct pronouns and verbs in past and present tense. Children enjoy dramatic play and make-believe. They become curious about the written appearance of language and like reading stories about home and community. Let children act out stories, and write out the child's stories so they can see the words in print.

Summary: Parents should read to their children at levels of their understanding and beyond. Engage children in conversation, modeling sentence structure, and language. Parents should help their children explore their world with language, games, toys, and environmental contact. Parents should tell stories to their children and have physical contact with them.

Parents should supply children with a variety of opportunities to observe, explore, reason, discuss, and experiment. Hide and Seek books such as *I Spy* are very useful and children enjoy them.

Children need help learning to be emotionally stable and interacting appropriately with other people and the environment. Parents should set boundaries, rules, and disciplines that are appropriate for their child. Parents should use opportunities for discussion, listen to their child, and give guidance. Encourage the child to try new things, but continue to support them even if they fail. Avoid being overly critical. Create safe and secure opportunities. Give children space to discover themselves.

Resources: Picture books with high quality illustrations and some words in print. Use repetitive and rhythmic phrases. Books should contain words and pictures of actions and objects familiar to the child. Use books that allow for visual, physical, and auditory stimulation, and books about the child's family and environment.

School Readiness: A child who develops these early skills will be more ready for school opportunities. These are the building blocks upon which other language develops. Not having these skills and going to school unprepared with them would be like building a house without a foundation. It just would not stand. Early childcare centers, day cares, nursery schools, and baby sitters cannot replace parent and child interaction. Certainly, they are better than nothing. Still, we need to help our young parents become their child's first resource in life and not allow the cycle of someone else's control to continue.

Educational preparedness and life readiness needs to begin at home.

1. *Cognitive Development*: Memory, reasoning, reflection, insight, anticipation, perception, and concepts.

    - "Children who grow up without a variety of experiences may be three to five years behind other children in developing mental strategies that aid recall." (Donna Norton, *Through the Eyes of a Child*, 1999.)
    - Age 2-3: Children find new ways to organize and classify their world. They begin to remember two to three items on a list. Parents can engage children in simple chores such as picking up and putting away their toys. The caregiver should provide opportunities to discuss and group by color, size, shape, and usage. The child exercises short-term memory.
    - Age 3-4: Children understand the relationship of things to each other, and how things belong together. They enjoy making things, and sort by number and amount and bigger and smaller. Give the child matching games such as picture puzzles and opportunities to group by size and color. Supply picture-counting books that allow children to count objects and compare sizes.
    - Age 4-5: The child can remember to do up to three things asked of them. They can retell a story. The child's ability to group things by sight increases and they pretend to tell time. However, the child does not understand the concepts "now" and "before now."
    - Provide opportunities to listen to short stories and allow them to retell them. Use visual aides for stories such as felt boards and pictures. Have children practice following three step directions and give the child additional opportunities for classifying objects. Add touch and use to the classification of sight. Read stories that include time in the theme, such as seasons, times of day, and days of the week.

2. *Motor Skills*: We cannot always assume that children will learn to hold, pick up and assemble objects, and tie their shoes before reaching or graduating from kindergarten. Occasionally, children need special

attention from physical and occupational therapists for learning to walk, sit, and hold things properly. Sometimes medical disabilities exist. Additionally, leaving a child in a crib, carriage, or highchair for long periods without the opportunity to use developed skills can lead to delayed development.

Early childhood games such as patty-cake, mom and dad crawling on the floor with baby, walking baby by the hands, and ring-around-the-rosy help develop motor skills and can easily be incorporated in a storytelling session. The side effects of these interactions include language development, bonding, and laughter. This early attention does not guarantee that there will be no physical developmental problems, especially if a child is genetically prone to a disability, however it can help with early motor skill development. The skills of walking and running are developed before the child can hold small objects. Fine motor skills take longer to develop, which is why toys for young children are often larger than life.

3. *Language Development*

Stories, Games, and Songs: A list of nursery rhymes is found on page (72). These rhymes and other forms of repetitive story or song help develop memory skills crucial to sustained education. They also offer opportunities for words to be repeated in context, which allows the brain to begin forming a word base and comprehension. The child will begin to understand that saying "Run Baby Run" rather than "Baby Run Baby" is correct. Songs can make it easier to recall words because the tune acts as a framework that the words must fit, triggering memory. Games allow time for interaction, physical activity, and the beginnings of social behavior skills, such as the following:

- *Personality Development*: Our way of reacting to other people, places, things, and events. This will depend on early experiences.
- *Learning to express* proper emotions, experience empathy, and develop self-esteem.

- *Overcoming fears*, learning to trust, relinquishing the need to have ones own way, and learning acceptable forms of interaction with peers and adults.

4. *Trusting versus Mistrust*: Children are good at reading facial expression while still infants. They will eventually understand the subtlety in language, like knowing our teammate from the opposition.
5. *Autonomy versus Shame or Doubt*: Follow the crowd or go off on our own, independent work or teamwork.

- Initiative versus Guilt: learn when it is appropriate to make individual decisions.
- Age 1-2: The child is very much dependent on the outside world to meet their needs. Their identity is completely tied to the caregiver.
- Age 2-3: Develop identity separately from other family members, but still feel a need for security. The adult should provide support of individual identities and self-worth, and hold a child to give them a sense of security especially during lap reading.
- Age 3-4: A steady self-concept. The child begins to identify him or herself as "I" and has set feelings about themselves. They need warm and secure environments to withdraw from unhappy situations. The child may suggest that problems do not exist or blame someone else. They become more aware of their cultural heritage. Adults should provide opportunities to let children know we care about them, make them feel accepted and worthy, create a warm reading place in the home, and give guidance to help children accept mistakes. Read literature that helps a child become proud of their identity, cultural heritage, home, and neighborhood.
- Age 4-5: Children continue to be egocentric, believing the world exists to serve them. They talk in first-person as center of the world. The child will improve their ability to handle emotions appropriately, while fear of the unknown can cause them to lose self-confidence and control of emotion. Children begin to respond to outside moti-

vation such as making a mommy happy or pleasing teacher. This is a move away from ego-centralism. However, the child still needs a warm, secure environment.

Provide literature where a child can identify with a character. Help them identify positive ways to react to problems. Adults should use books that talk about emotions, help children understand new concepts, and feel comfortable with their ability to handle unknown situations. Find opportunities to observe and read about good role-models.

6. *Social Development*: Acquire beliefs, values, and behaviors.

- Age 2-3: Children imitate actions and behaviors. They play make-believe.

  Adults can provide role-playing activities so the child views things from another's perspective. Provide toys and objects that can be used creatively such as pots and wooden spoons, cardboard boxes, blocks, and nondescript items. While many of today's toys are lovely and interesting, many do too much for the child, leaving little room for imagination.

- Age 3-4: The child realizes that others have feelings too. They like playing with other children and get attached to other children. Children enjoy group activities and group games. They are mindful of the ability to identify feelings by watching facial expressions.

  Caregivers should provide opportunities to talk about feelings, encourage sharing, taking turns, and cooperative play. Let children be both leaders and followers in games and group activities. Encourage them to be sensitive about the feelings of others.

- Age 4-5: Children begin to avoid aggression when angry and look for other ways to solve the problems. They can be frequently bossy, assertive, and use excuses. They begin to understand consequences of good and bad and use attention-seeking behavior. Children at this age seldom play alone, but prefer to do work related activities such as building blocks by themselves. The child has an increased awareness of roles people play such as teacher, nurse, doctor, and firefighter. The child may exhibit unreasonable fears of the dark, thunder, and animals.

Adults provide praise for correct behavior. Help children calm down and talk about the situation. Direct them to finding a solution and explain actions so they can understand them and discuss alternatives. Encourage persistence so the child completes tasks. This is crucial for problem-solving and self-directed learning. Provide opportunities to meet different kinds of people through live experiences or in books. Supply materials and opportunities for dramatic role-play. Find ways to help children overcome their fears by sharing stories that act as models of how others overcame their fears.

Implications: Children need guidance to explore and solve everyday problems and crisis. Children need opportunities to play with others, role-play, and be alone at times of work. They need to be encouraged to complete tasks.

SESSION VIII

Parents tell stories to their children. Refreshments follow the session. It is nice to give the families two or three books if you can buy them or get them donated. Also, you may want to supply the parents with a button or certificate showing their completion of the program. If any show a real interest in continuing to study storytelling, you should give them leads to local and national organizations that can support their interest.

MOMMY AND ME® SESSION HANDOUTS FOR PARENTS

The following handouts may be copied for parents. Feel free to amend them as needed for your participants or have them make notes in the space provided.

Also, please feel free to copy the list of stories and games that follows the parents' handouts. This will help the parents find stories to use during the program and later with their children.

Session III: Storytelling Basics

Scary Stories suggestions.

"Hansel and Gretel," Brothers Grimm

"The Ghost with One Black Eye," Priscilla Howe, *The Ghost with One Black Eye and Other Stories*

Notes: ______________________________

____

____

____

____

Stories with a moral lesson:

"Being Greedy Chokes Anansi," *Favorite Folktales from Around the World*, Jane Yolan.

"Two Friends: How They Parted," *The King's Drum*, Harold Courlander.

"The Boy Who Cried Wolf ," Aesop

Notes: ______________________________

____

____

____

____

Silly and Nonsense suggestions:

Nursery Rhymes

Going on a Bear Hunt, Michael Rosen, Walker Books.

Notes: ______________________________

____

____

____

____

Session IV: Continued Storytelling Basics

Story Length:

Pre K-K: 5-10 min per story, 20-30 min per program.

Gr. 1-2: 5-20 min per story, 45-60 minute per program

Gr. 3-12: 5-20 minutes per story, 45-60 min per program.

Grade 7-adult can also sit for stories that are 30-40 minutes or longer if the story is relevant.

Notes: ____

____

____

____

____

Additional Notes: ______________________________________

____

____

____

____

Methods of Delivery:

Props: felt boards, puppets, objects such as examples from a story, picture books half read/half told.

Additional Aids for Engaging Listeners

1. Repetition
2. Participation
3. Song and Music
4. Costume

Notes: ____

____

____

____

____

____

SESSION VI AND VII

The Importance of Telling Stories:

Early Literacy

LANGUAGE DEVELOPMENT: read aloud books, repetition, rhyme, simple phrases, games such as Peek-a-boo and Patty Cake, action picture books, experiences such as walks in the park or neighborhood. Nursery rhymes.

- Age one: Children speak their first words. Do not understand hidden objects.
- Age 18 months: Children form sentences such as "baby sleep," "milk gone," "see mommy."
- Age two: Two-word combinations.
- Age three: The child may have learned as many as nine hundred words. They have added adverbs, pronouns, prepositions and adjectives.
- Age four: Children can make grammatically correct sentences. They begin to question why and how. A child may have fifteen hundred words. Do not understand tense such as past, present, future.
- Age 5-6: Children acquire words faster and may have as many as six thousand. They understand complex sentences, and use correct pronouns and verbs in past and present tense. Children enjoy dramatic play and make-believe. Curious about the written appearance of language and like reading stories about home and community.

Notes: ____

____

____

____

____

____

____

School Readiness

A child who develops these early skills will be more ready for school opportunities. Give children as many experiences in their homes and communities as possible. Talk to them, ask questions and teach them to ask questions. Let them touch and play, hear and see in safe environments to strengthen:

1. Cognitive Development: Memory, reasoning, reflection, insight, anticipation, perception, and concepts.

    ✦ Age 2-3: Children begin to remember two to three items on a list, do simple chores, discuss and group by color, size, shape, and usage.

    ✦ Age 3-4: Children enjoy making things, sort and match by number and amount, and bigger and smaller.

    ✦ Age 4-5: The child can remember to do up to three things asked of them. They can retell a story.

2. Motor Skills

    Early childhood games such as patty-cake, mom and dad crawling on the floor with baby, walking baby by the hands, and ring-around-the-rosy help develop motor skills.

3. Personality Development: Our way of reacting to other people, places, things, and events.

    ✦ Age 1-2: The child is very much dependent on the outside world to meet their needs.

    ✦ Age 2-3: Develop identity separate from other family members, but still feel a need for security.

    ✦ Age 3-4: A steady self-concept. The child begins to identify him or herself as "I" and has set feelings about themselves. They need warm and secure environments to withdraw from unhappy situations.

    Children become more aware of their cultural heritage. Read literature that helps a child become proud of their identity, cultural heritage, home, and neighborhood.

    ✦ Age 4-5: Children continue to be egocentric, believing the world exists to serve them.

Children begin to respond to outside motivation such as making a mommy happy or pleasing teacher.

4. Social Development: Acquire beliefs, values, and behaviors.

    - Age2-3: Children imitate actions and behaviors. They play make-believe.
    - Age 3-4: The child realizes that others have feelings too. They like playing with other children and get attached to other children.
    - Age 4-5: Children begin to avoid aggression when angry and look for other ways to solve the problems. They can be frequently bossy, assertive, and use excuses. They begin to understand consequences of good and bad and use attention-seeking behavior.

Notes: ____

____

____

____

____

____

Mommy and Me® Stories, Activities and Rhyme Suggestions

Ages Pre K:

- Touch Play
- Patty Cake: Making mud cakes or some edible art
- This is the Way the Gentlemen Ride
- Tickle Time: just taking time to play tickle is a wonderful way to bond with your child.
- Round and Round the Garden
- Peek-a-Boo
- Raspberry Bellies: blowing on baby's belly
- Rock-a-Bye Baby
- This Little Piggy
- This is Baby's: naming body parts
- Piggy back, shoulder rides, and swinging arms
- Motor Play
- This is the House that Jack Built: with Building blocks
- The Three Little Pigs: with Building Blocks
- Itsy Bitsy Spider
- Counting Play
- One Two Buckle My Shoe
- One Little, Two Little, Three Little . . .
- Alice the Camel
- Language and Imagination Play
- Naming Objects
- Playing house, tea party etc.

Age 4-6:

- Language and Imagination Play
- Short finger plays, rhymes, and five-minute stories.
- Little Bunny Foo Foo
- Going on a Bear Hunt: may also be used with age two & three.
- "Ghost with One Black Eye" (Priscilla Howe) see bibliography

Age 7-12:

Language and Imagination Play

The stories are too numerous to mention, but they can be longer and more complex as children get older. We should not forget that these older children also need to retain their sense of the imaginative. Imagination is a key component to problem solving.

Other activities to consider include:

- Family rituals and family stories that help give children a sense of purpose and belonging. Encourage these special activities whenever possible. Family rituals can be as simple as a set time for reading a story. These ritual times include activities before bed, a special food that mom is best at preparing and serves at certain times each week or at special family holiday celebrations. Bath time rituals or a parent coming home are wonderful opportunities for family connections. Family stories may include "What I was doing the day you were born" or "I remember a time when Grandmother came to visit." These are the things children will remember years later and pass on to their children. They are very important to identity building.
- Personal Rituals are empowering and wonderful for children of all ages including young adults. Pulling daisy petals, "stamping," saying "Starlight, Star Bright," and wishing on ladybugs are among many common personal rituals.
- Disgusting or nonsensical rhymes may be distasteful to adults, but children love them. They make language fun and show many nuances in the child's native language they may not get otherwise. Some rhymes seem to make no sense at all, but to a child they are quite precious. When children experiment with these things they learn the power of words. They have fun with word play and innuendo and begin to enjoy the sound of language. Children see how words can affect others. Here are some examples.

  Little Bunny Foo Foo
  The Hearse Song

Great Green Gobs
Alice the Camel
I One the Sandbox
Tongue Twisters and most Nursery Rhymes

If putting boundaries on the use of these stories and songs is necessary, parents can explain when they are or are not appropriate. However, Children are usually adept at figuring this out themselves, based on adult reaction.

- Group games. Learning to play with other children is crucial for learning to be cooperative. Children learn to follow rules and instructions. They learn about various roles and their world.

  The Farmer in the Dell
  Follow the Leader
  Simon Says
  Tag

- Choosing "IT" becomes an interest for children as young as age three. They begin to learn about followers and leaders. There are many games for deciding who will be "IT."

  One Potato
  Eenie Meenie
  Engine Engine Number Nine

- Dexterity is enhanced by finger games.

  Here is the Church
  One Little, Two Little, Three Little Indians
  Where is Thumbkin
  Shadow Puppets

- Cause and Effect

  Understanding this concept will help children make decisions throughout their lives. Things as simple as setting up blocks or dominoes and toppling them enhance this understanding.

- Naming Body Parts

  Heads and Shoulders, Knees and Toes
  This is Baby's . . .

- Family Play can be as simple as sitting on the floor and rolling a ball to a small child, playing hide and seek, water-fights, or making believe. Adults can give the child "Horse back" and "Piggy back" rides.

- Songs: The following is a list of traditional songs that have crossed generations and often involve hand gesture and other physical activity. Many children's songs are build-ons and strengthen memory.

  I've Been Workin' on the Railroad
  Ring-Around The Rosy
  Rock-a-Bye Baby
  Pop Goes the Weasel
  Go Tell Aunt Rhody
  Skip to My Lou
  Froggie Went a Courtin'
  Yankee Doodle
  She'll Be Comin' Round the Mountain
  I'm a Little Teapot
  Old MacDonald Had a Farm
  It's Raining, It's Pouring
  Row, Row, Row, Your Boat
  This Old Man
  London Bridge
  Hush Little Baby
  Twinkle Twinkle Little Star

- Nursery Rhymes:

    Hot Cross Buns
    Little Jack Horner
    One Two Buckle My Shoe
    House That Jack Built
    Jack Be Nimble
    Three Little Kittens
    Pease Porridge Hot
    Little Bo Peep
    There Was an Old Woman Who Lived in A Shoe
    Crooked Man
    Little Boy Blue

BIBLIOGRAPHY FOR MOMMY AND ME®

Allison, Christine. *I'll Tell You a Story, I'll Sing You a Song*. New York: Bantam Doubleday Dell. 1987.

Cobb, Vicki. *Arts and Crafts You Can Eat*. New York: J.B. Lippincott.

Martin, Elaine. *Kids' Games: A parent's guide to playing with your three to six-year-old*. Canada: Random House. 1989.

Masi & Leiderman. *Baby Play*. USA: Creative Publishing. 2001.

Masi. *Toddler Play*. USA: Creative Publishing. 2001.

Moore, Vardine. *Pre-School Story Hour*. New York: Scarecrow Press. 1966.

Redleaf, Rhoda. *Open the Door and Let's Explore*. St. Paul: Toys and Things Press. 1983.

Read Alouds:

Brown, Margaret Wise. *Goodnight Moon*. Harper and Row. 1947.

Brown, Ruth. *Copycat*. Dutton Children's Books. 1994.

Cane, Eric. *The Very Hungry Caterpillar*. New York: Collins. 1970.

Carle, Eric. *Today is Monday*. Philomel. 1993.

Dr. Seuss : Random House.(any of these are wonderful. *One Fish, Two Fish* is great for young Children.)

Ehlert, Lois. *Fish Eyes*. Red Wagon Books. 1990.

Howe, Priscilla. *The Ghost with One Black Eye and Other Stories.*_www.storyteller.net. (Audio recording.)

Hubbell, Patricia. *Pots and Pans*. Harper Collins. 1998.

Keats, Ezra Jack. *The Snowy Day*. New York: Viking. 1962.

Leaf, Munro. *The Story of Ferdinand*. New York: Viking. 1936.

McCloskey, Roberta. *Make Way for Ducklings*. New York: Viking. 1941.

Rey, Hans A. *Curious George*. Houghton Mifflin. 1941.

Rylant, Cynthia. *The Relatives Came*. Simon and Schuster. 1985.

Sendak, Maurice. *Where the Wild Things Are*. Harper and Row. 1963.

Scott, William R. *Caps For Sale*. William Scott, Inc. 1940.

Wiesner, David. *Tuesday*. Clarion Books. 1991. (Has no words, but is great for making up your own stories)

Wood, Audrey. *Silly Sally*. Harcourt Brace and Company.

Wellington, Monica. *Baby Goes Shopping*. Dutton Children's Books. 1997. (No story, but a wonderful book for young children to learn to label objects.)

STORIES OF CHOICE AND EMPOWERMENT

The goal of this curriculum is to introduce the youth to story structure and ways in which metaphor is used in stories. At-risk teens often find it easier to tell their stories through their artwork and in tales told from a different point of view. This program will enable them to tell their own stories and better understand the power of stories they hear.

This eight-session curriculum begins with an introduction of the program and ends with a wrap-up celebration. "Breaking bread" together in celebration is a communal activity and sets a good example of how community members come together in support of each other. It is very important to stress this togetherness.

Note: Sessions can be lengthened or shortened and these are designed to be one to two hours in length. Length will depend on the facility and the capability of the youth to work together. Sometimes it is necessary to make groups smaller and time shorter.

Number of youth per group should not exceed 12-15 and for best results can be smaller but not less than three.

Session One: Trust Building

Take this time to get to know a little about each youth and let them know a little about you as group leader.

Materials: yarn and scissors

1. Visit with the youth: Ice-breaker activity. See Yarn activity. Have teens say their names and one thing about themselves that makes them special. Some youth will not be able to say something nice about themselves and may not feel comfortable speaking. This is a good time to start building trust by not forcing them to speak. Unsolicited, other youth may suggest things they like about the person. You can also encourage him to speak his name by telling him that you want to make sure he is part of the group and ties his yarn into the group ball. "You are important to me."
2. Tell them a story that will give them a sense of what to expect over the next seven sessions. Suggested story: "Sir Gawain and Dame Ragnell."[4]

[4] "Sir Gwain and Dame Ragnell" can be found on page 7 of *Dancing at the Crossroads: Stories and Activities for At-Risk Youth Programs.*

3. Explain the program objective: To develop a story about them.

4. Explain next session's activity. "To begin understanding the power of story through metaphor."

V. Close group (See closing examples on page 41).

Session Two: Pre Evaluation and Discussion of Metaphor

Materials: Evaluation forms (Appendix IV), pencils, handouts on metaphors and story structure (Appendix II), chart paper, tape, marker, yarn, scissors, or materials for another activity if you choose one.

1. Handout Pre Evaluation forms and ask youth to complete them. This is not necessary but may be helpful to you. You may also wish to create an evaluation of your own.

2. Explain Goal: To create our own stories using metaphor and symbolism.

   a. Ask the youth what they know about metaphor.

   b. Create a working metaphor and symbols sample-list for the group (See examples in Appendix I. Archetypes on page 117).

3. Tell a story with metaphors. (Suggestion: Use Crossroad's version of "Hansel and Gretel" from *Dancing at the Crossroads: A Guide for Caregivers in At-Risk Youth Programming.*)

   A. Ask the youth to name the metaphors in the story and add these to the list.

   B. Discuss the possible meanings for the story metaphors. Be sure to let the teens lead the discussion as each listener may understand the story on a personal level.

4. Yarn Activity: Teens name objects that represent them metaphorically.

5. Explain next session's activity. (Game: Battle of Evermore)

6. Close group.

Session Three: Game "The Battle of Evermore" by Lorna Czarnota.

Materials: chart paper, marker, an inflatable world globe or ball.

1. Divide into three groups: good, evil, and neutral characters. The neutral characters should consist of an odd number, possibly three. These will be the judges for the game. The odd number allows for tie-breaking.
2. Each youth, and support-staff if they choose to participate, will choose an animal character they believe fits with the metaphor of good and evil, depending on their team.

   For example, Fox might be an evil character because foxes are sly and tricky. Wise Owl and Peaceful Dove make good judges. The teens may have different opinions than the group leader about what makes a character good or evil. It is more important for them to have a personal connection with the character than for them to feel the same way on this issue.

   A. Write the characters and the teen's name for each on chart paper.

   B. Choose a side to begin.

   C. The first player approaches the judges and explains, in character, why their team should inherit the world. Some youth will feel uncomfortable doing this. Let them find their own time and way of approaching the challenge.

   D. Judges deliberate. If they agree, they give the world to that player. If they disagree, the world remains where it is.

   E. The teams take turns until each person has taken a turn. It requires at least nine people to play this game. If there are fewer or they wish to continue playing, they may be given second or third turns using the same characters or by developing new ones.

   F. Conclude the game: Either good or evil will win the game, depending on which team has the world when everyone has taken their turns. Presenter should finish by saying, "The world is

> constantly moving from one side to the other. Sometimes it seems very good, sometimes evil. We make a difference. Everything we do matters."

This game has been played with at-risk and special needs youth. They have passed the world from good to evil. It has resided in both places. However, in most situations, the teens are very disappointed when evil inherits the world. They truly want it to be good.

3. Explain next session's activity. (Telling our own stories. "If a reporter interviews you, what will the headline of your story be?")
4. Close group.

Session Four: Begin Story Development

Materials: yarn and scissors.

1. Story Starter question: "If a reporter were to write an article about you, what would the headline be?" Have the teens hold their answers until you give your example.
2. Tell a story about something that happened in your life. How difficult your story is will be determined by the abilities and status of your listeners. When working with trauma survivors it is okay to tell a tough story as long as safety is foremost, trust has been built, and staff support is in place. Share your headline. "My headline is…"
3. Youth share their headlines and attach their yarn to the "story ball." Never force them to share. Allow them to attach their yarn, nonetheless. If they are reluctant to tie into the story ball, ask permission to do it for them. In this way, that reluctant teen sees that he is valued.
4. Explain next session's activity. "Choose an event in your life and share it as if it happened to someone else."

   Another optional activity is "Truth or Lie." The teen's story must have something true in it. They can add one or more lies or keep it completely true. The group tries to guess what is real and what is not.

If you have an unruly group that doesn't like to listen, this activity can keep their attention.

5. Close group.

Session Five: Share our Stories.

Materials: yarn and scissors.

1. Each person shares the story they have worked on over the week and attaches their yarn to the story ball.
2. The group leader will tell a story of empowerment and follow up with a discussion.
3. Explain next session's art activity and reinforce the goal of having a ceremony on the last night with shared stories.
4. Close group.

Session Six: Story and Art Activity

Materials: Will vary with the activity, should include yarn and scissors.

1. Open the session with a question relating to the story the group leader will tell this week. Teens may give answers and attach their yarn.
2. The group leader will tell a story that leads into an art activity.
3. Create follow-up art. For example, if the group leader tells the story of "Sir Gawain and the Green Knight,"[5] the youth may make green belts as the follow-up or for "Vassalisa"[5] make dolls. Masks or wish boxes may be suitable for almost any story. It may take two or more sessions to complete this artwork so make sure to package that into your planning. (See individual stories for suggested activities.)
4. Collect art to display on the last night. Do not let the youth keep their artwork or it may not be available for the final presentation.

[5]"Sir Gawain and the Green Knight" and "Vassalisa" can be found in *Dancing at the Crossroads: Activities and Stories for At-Risk Youth Programs*.

Session Seven: Story with Art Activity

Materials: Will vary with the activity, yarn, and scissors, and evaluation forms (Appendix IV).

1. Open with a question or statement relating to the proposed story for this session. Allow each person to say something and attach his or her yarn to the story ball.
2. Tell a story.
3. Create follow-up art. Bead making is a creative way for teens to award a gift to their sponsors on the last night or finish artwork from the previous session. (Appendix V: Materials Resource List.)
4. Collect art for the last night. Have youth fill out post evaluation forms and collect them
5. Remind youth that they can invite a sponsor or staff person to attend our last session. Check with the facility in advance for permission to do this.
6. Close circle.

Session Eight: Last Session, Rite of Passage Ceremony

Materials: food and drinks for celebration, table set with a candle, shell, flowers, rock, chime, table cloth, strung beads for the youth, beads for their staff person, youth artworks, yarn, and scissors.

1. The group leader will tell a brief sample story.
2. Give the youth a chance to tell their stories and attach their yarn.
3. Give each youth a strung bead and let the youth award their sponsor. "As long as we tell our stories, we honor ourselves. You have finished this program and the beads you receive will remind you to keep telling your stories. These beads represent your success and completion of this program."
4. Present the story ball to the group or staff member as something they can continue after this program is finished. Return their artworks.

Rite of Passage Ceremony

The following outline is just a suggestion for a ceremony at the end of the eight sessions.

Note on serving food: Teens like to eat. Check with the facility first for dietary requirements and permission to have food.

1. Explain Purpose: To mark the accomplishment of this group and to remind the youth to keep telling their stories.
2. Light Candle: Sometimes this may have to be a ceremonial lighting without actually lighting the candle. Check with the facility for fire codes or use LED lights. (Appendix V: Materials Resource List.)
3. Sound Chime: This sets the time apart from the rest of the session and the rest of the day. It creates an atmosphere of something special.
4. Youth share their stories.
5. The group leader will tell "Star Woman's Basket" or another appropriate story.
6. Make Wishes: Give each youth a strip of paper and a pen. If you told the story of Star Woman, remind the youth that her trust was betrayed but you promise to keep the youths' wishes in a safe place.

   One suggestion for collecting wishes is to place the paper strips in a round basket, as in the story. Keeping promises to these young people is important so having a plan for when the basket gets full is advisable. The wishes might be buried in a garden "to help good things grow" or can be hung on a "wish tree" to disintegrate naturally. Burning usually represents ridding oneself of something and would not be appropriate for this activity. (See Wish Planting Ceremony with the story "Star Woman's Basket," *Dancing at the Crossroads: Stories and Activities in At-Risk Youth Programs.*)

   As each youth places a wish in the basket invite him or her to speak that wish out loud. Explain that speaking it is like a commitment and brings it closer to fruition. Never force them to share however, remind them they can keep it private if they choose. If you have a chime for them to ring, they can do so now.

7. Present award beads on a string to each youth. Use Fimo Clay to make your own beads or purchase them at your local craft shop. (Appendix V: Materials Resource List.)
8. Close Circle
9. EAT. Breaking bread is an important social interaction for closure. You may ask the youth what they would like for their snacks but always confirm with the agency.

MY STORY/MY POEM®: A CLUB FOR YOUTH VOICES

The purpose of the youth club is to give youth an opportunity for self-expression and to validate and honor their stories. This eight-session program will culminate with a collection of youth poems and stories. Obtaining permission from the facility may be necessary due to confidentiality policies if you plan to have something printed. It is possible to do this using false names.

Session One: Introduction and Trust Building

Materials: heavy books for each person, folders, journals, pens, chart paper, marker, sample poems, audio recorder, scissors, evaluation forms (Appendix IV.), poem examples of your choice.

1. Open the circle: name activity
    A. Youths say their names and one thing that is unique about them.
    B. Tie yarn to the "story ball."
2. Fill out pre-session evaluation forms and hand them in. (See Appendix IV)
3. Group Leader will review rules and guidelines for participation.
    A. Have the youth help determine what these rules will be, unless the facility already has house rules.
4. Review the purpose of this club: To give the youth a voice and publish a book of their works at the end. Give the youth their journals and folders.
5. The group leader will tell a story.

6. The youth will share some of their ideas for sessions during the program. There will be an opportunity to use some of their ideas in Session Six.
7. Discuss whether the youth have any favorite poets and read two or three poems chosen by the group leader.
8. Explain the power of the spoken word and how some ancient Celtic poets and storytellers learn their materials.
   A. It took many years to learn thousands of pieces that had to be memorized and passed on orally.
   B. The students met with their teacher and were given assignments to learn for the following day.
   C. The students lie on the floor in a darkened, quiet room with a heavy rock on their chests. This rock kept their minds focused.
   D. The students meditated on the theme until a poem came to them. They shared this poem during their next lesson. Again this was done completely from memory without writing it down, as early people had no written language.
9. "Rock" activity: give each youth a heavy book and ask them to place it on their chest while lying on the floor. The youth will be given a poetry topic and compose a simple two-line rhyming poem on that topic. When they have finished, they will return quietly to their seats and the group will share the poems.
   A. Some teens will not want to participate in this activity due to trust issues. Do not force them to lie down or close their eyes if they are not comfortable with this.
   B. The youths will journal their stories after sharing orally. Those who do not wish to share may write theirs in the journal. Explain that these journals will be collected at the end of the seventh session to prepare the book for publication. They may feel free to write anything they like in their journals, as they will mark the pages they want the presenter to read.
   C. Allow a few minutes to write any additional thoughts in the journal.

10. Youth may decorate club folders with their names. These will hold any handouts given to the teens. The group leader will collect the folders each session.

11. Any remaining time will be used to share. If preferred, the group leader will tell another story.

12. Wrap up: explain the goal of our next meeting and close the circle.

Session Two: Where Stories and Poems Come From

Materials: Storytelling books and recordings, chart paper, marker, CD/tape-player, and chime

1. Open the circle (see page 37): Observation activity

   Purpose: To strengthen ability to observe visually and verbally describe the observation. To take a moment to truly look at another person without fear.

   A. Pair the youth into groups of two. Partners face each other.
   B. Group leader gives them time to observe each other, looking at everything they are wearing and how they are wearing it.
   C. Partners turn backs on each other and change up to three appropriate items they are wearing. These may be removed, switched, or worn in a different way.
   D. On the group leader's chime signal, the partners face each other again and try to figure out what three items they changed.
   E. The group shares their observations and feelings during the activity.

2. Sound Observation Activity.

   Purpose: To strengthen the use of listening for observation. This activity can be done indoors or outside

   A. The teens sit comfortably and close their eyes.
   B. On the chime signal, they may open their eyes and write the sounds they heard in their journals.
   C. Youth may count these items and share with the group to see who heard the most.

3. Youth may share anything they have written during the session such as ideas or things that happened.
4. Discuss where writers and poets find ideas for stories and poems.
   A. Observation of people, things, sounds, sights, and occurrences in daily life.
   B. Sometimes these are turned into fantasies. Sometimes they are very realistic.
5. Group leader tells a sample story "Moth to the Flame."

   (See the story and follow-up discussions in *Dancing at the Crossroads: Stories and Activities for At-Risk Youth Programs*).
6. Show the youth the storytelling books and recordings. Allow time for viewing.
7. Outdoor exploration. This should take no more than five to ten minutes. Challenge: find something outside that inspires a poem or story, and write about it in the journal.
8. Journal sharing. Youth may read anything they have written from this session or during the week.
9. Wrap Up: Goal of next meeting and close the circle.

Session Three: How are Poems and Stories Different or Alike?

Materials: chart paper, marker, Illustration cards or large tarot cards (Appendix V: Materials Resource List), poster board, pencils, rulers, colored markers, scissors, old magazines, glitter, glue, and assortment of odds-n-ends (feathers, buttons, etc.) Storytelling books and recordings, and CD/tape-player

1. Open the Circle: "If you could be anything, what would you be?"

   Purpose: Using Metaphor and Archetypes.

   A. Besides sharing their answers to the question, the youth may share anything they have written over the week.

2. Discuss the structure of poem and story.
   A. Stories have a beginning, middle, and end that takes a character or characters through a plot completely.
   B. Poems look at one moment or a feeling related to a moment in time.
3. Compile a club list of metaphor and archetypes that include characters, colors, and other symbols. (See Appendix I for additional ideas.)
4. Share illustration or tarot cards as story starters. Tarot cards are a wonderful source for many symbols that can lead to a story. However, some people have an aversion to their use. Check with the facility beforehand.
5. Using poster board, craft materials, and the list of metaphors and archetypes, youth design their own Illustration cards. These should answer one of the following questions.

   "If you could be anything, what would you be?"

   "Who are you?"

   "Who would you like to be in ten years?"
6. Youths journal a story or poem about their illustration card and share what they have created.
7. Fill remaining time with a story or a recording.
8. Wrap up: discuss goal of next meeting and close the circle.

Session Four: Putting our Own Events Into Poem and Story

Materials: Materials: rolls adding machine paper for individual timelines, one heavy book per person, chart paper, markers, stickers of various kinds for labeling events, storytelling books and recordings, CD/tape-player.

1. Open circle (see page 37) : Personal timeline

   Purpose: Record events that can be considered positively or negatively significant. "Each event in our lives changes the course we take and becomes part of who we are."

   A. Each teen will create a timeline of events on their rolled paper. They should begin with their birth date and label each event with a title and date if known. Some youth may have difficulty putting some events in writing. They can use stickers instead.

   B. If the youth finish and are waiting for others, they can add future events such as a graduation, wedding, or occupation.

   C. Youth share their timelines and anything they have written during the week.

2. Discuss the idea of story as a model for living. Discuss how poems encapsulate a moment in time.

3. Youth choose one place on their timeline. They may need to break an event down to a specific moment.

4. Use the "Rock" activity on page 84 to help the teens write a poem about their chosen moment.

5. Youth journal and share what they have created.

6. Discuss the use of beginning, middle, and end in a story.

7. Goal: Write a story based on a chosen moment, then place the poem inside the new story. This is something they should do for homework during the week.

8. Wrap up: Next session's goal and close the circle.

Session Five: Developing our Stories

Materials: Chart paper, marker, storytelling books and recordings, and CD/tape player.

1. Open circle: Once there was a...(youth fill in the blank using themselves. Ex. "Once there was a girl who was lost in the jungle." Let them expand on these during this session.)

   Purpose: To create a personal story as if it happened to someone else as another option for story writing.

2. Youths listen to a personal story with a poem told by the group leader and discuss how to make it into a third person story.
3. Youth share anything they have written over the week.
4. Finish any loose ends from the previous session. Give the youth time to work on their story/poems.
5. Let the youths share their ideas in groups of two.
6. *Activity*: The youth will share one story they heard someone else tell. They should not give away who told the story. (Do this only if confidentiality can be maintained.)

   Purpose: To show another source for story.

7. Fill extra time with story, poem, or recording.
8. Wrap up and close circle

Session Six: A Youth-Driven Session.

Use one or more youth ideas to create this week's session. Fill in the outline for yourself.

- ✦ Materials:
- ✦ Open Circle:
- ✦ Close Circle: remind the youth that journals will be collected at the next meeting.

Session Seven: The Power of Imagination: Wearing the Mask

Purpose: To create an artwork and give the youth another way of telling a story.

Materials: chart paper, marker, mask materials, sample masks, mask video (Appendix V: Materials Resource List.), hand mirror, Post-its, post evaluation forms, pencils, storytelling books, recordings, and CD/tape player

1. Open circle (see page 37): Mirror activity

   Purpose: Another way to help youth connect with their bodies and use their imaginations.

   A. Youth will look into the mirror and decide who they want to be today. Journal their ideas or discuss them (depending on the needs of the youth, many do not like to write.) "Who did they see?" This is not an activity about physical appearances. It is about the inner person.

2. Group leader will tell a self-image story or play a recording. Suggested story for this session is "The Black Prince" found in *Dancing at the Crossroads: A Guide for Caregivers in At-Risk Youth Programming.* (See activities for this story in *Dancing at the Crossroads: Stories and Activities for At-Risk Youth Programs.*)

3. Youth share any thoughts about the story.

4. Discuss the masks people wear and how different cultures use masks. Some cultures believe that the mask is a living spirit and the person wearing it becomes that spirit. Some people use masks to hide their true self.

5. Pass the hand mirror and ask each person to look in it in turn. Have the next person in line describe something positive that the last person has to offer the group, community, or society at-large. This is a good activity for positive peer interaction and builds self esteem and caring

6. Create masks:

   A. Youth should make a mask that represents the face they wear for others to see or who they wanted to be today.

B. Or create masks around the concept of creation itself. For example, ask the youth "if you were a god or goddess, what ability would you have and how would you use it to change the world?"

C. If time permits, they can decorate the outside as what they let others see, while they can design the inside as their true self.

7. Youth share their masks and how/why they made them as they did. This can be done the following session if they need more time.
8. Wrap up: Explain how we will use their masks on the last day to tell a story or recite a poem.
9. Youth choose one story or three poems from their journal to publish and mark them with a Post-it. Additional pieces can be allowed for smaller groups.
10. Collect journals.
11. Fill out post evaluations.
12. Close circle (see page 41).

Session Eight: Celebrate the Final Session With Stories, Poems, Masks, and Food

Materials: masks, youth's published books, youth journals, food, youth folders.

1. Open Circle:(see page 37) Youths share anything they have written during the week.
2. Performance pieces. Youth tell their stories or read their poems with the mask.
3. Words of congratulations from the group leader.
4. Hand out youth books and return journals and folders.
5. Close
6. Eat. Obtaining permission from the facility for food may be necessary. Consider inviting a guest speaker such as a local storyteller or poet.

The following are optional additional sessions if a longer program is desired. They would be presented before the final celebration shown above.

Stories and Poems as Creative Dramatics

Materials: chart paper, marker, audio recorder or video camera, simple story props, plots, index cards and a basket.

1. Open circle (see page 37): What does it look like to be me?
2. Generate group plot and character cards. (These cards are labeled with plots and characters for creating an improvised story),
3. Discuss the use of body language, facial expression, voice to portray story. Can these be used for poetry?
4. Each youth draws a card from the basket and using a simple form of charades, acts out that part. They may ask one other person from the group to help them.
5. Discuss the rules for Impressions: a game of mirroring issues through story and poetic drama.

   RULES: Select an issue.

   A. Choose people to play roles in the drama.

      a. The Players may say or do anything to represent the issue except touch another player.

      b. Players need to follow house rules about foul language or name calling.

   B. Observers and other players may not criticize the player acting out a role.

6. Close circle (see page 41).

Seeing the Poem

Materials: chart paper, marker, audio recorder or video camera, simple story props, plots, character cards, basket, collage materials including magazines, glue, scissors, poster board, other objects, and audio recordings of sample poems.

1. Open circle: What does a poem taste like? Look like? Sound like? Feel like? Smell like?
2. Listen to the recorded poems.
3. Discuss the answers to our opening questions for each poem.
4. Youth choose one poem of their own, another youth's, or one supplied by the presenter.
5. Create a collage expressing one way a poem may be experienced other than auditory.
6. Share creations.
7. If time permits, we will do some more creative dramas
8. Wrap up: Discuss next session.
9. Close circle (see page 41).

Designing our Publication

Materials: youth journals, sample publication, inflatable globe, chart paper, and markers.

1. Open circle (see page 37): What one or two things do you want to be remembered for?
2. Discuss title and format for publication.
3. Discuss artwork to be used in publication.
4. Each youth may choose one story or three poems for publication. Mark these in their journals with post it notes.
5. The group may share anything extra at this time.
6. If equipment is available, begin typing the stories and poems as a group, or if equipment is not available, use an inflatable globe to play "The Battle of Evermore" on page 78.
7. Wrap up: Discuss next session.

HEROQUEST®: THE HERO'S JOURNEY

HeroQuest® was originally designed for a group of twelve boys at a residential treatment facility as part of their summer programming. The girls at this facility had been receiving "My Story/My Poem" workshops, but it was determined that something specific to boys would be a better choice. HeroQuest® can easily be adapted for girls or mixed groups.

HeroQuest® is a program designed to help youth explore their inner heroes by identifying the qualities of the hero, discovering the value of community heroes and personal mentors, and defining community identity. The purpose of this program is to help youth develop a better understanding of the important contributions they can make to their communities.

The hero's journey story is filled with metaphor or archetypal characterization. To determine which stories to use in this curriculum, it is best to begin with some definition or description of what might be a hero's qualities. This discussion should also be part of session one with a group of youth, making certain everyone understands the purpose of the program.

Webster's dictionary defines a hero as "a mythological or legendary figure often of divine descent endowed with great strength or ability, an illustrious warrior, one that shows great courage, the principal male character in a literary or dramatic work, the central figure in an event, period, or movement."

The author uses the following interpretation. "Heroes are beings set apart from others by deeds, actions, and abilities. They will use these willingly, and sometimes unknowingly, to better the environments or lives of others. The hero-self often benefits as a side-effect, but some part of self is always sacrificed."

Whatever definition of hero is chosen, some elements are always found in traditional story. They are included as part of Session Two. Before beginning this program, the facilitator should decide on the stories to be told and the final project or ceremony which will act as a culminating celebration of the youths' journey through the program. This represents the hero's reward at the end of the journey. These factors will act as the framework for your session designs.

The curriculum is based on six to eight sessions of programming with additional sessions included for extended programming.

Session One: Introduction

Materials: Talking stick (See Appendix V), journals, folders, paper, pens, handouts, craft items to decorate folders.

1. Introduction and rule setting for participation in the group. Decide how you will establish ground rules and how you will introduce the program. Your introduction should include the participants saying their names and a description of the purpose of the sessions, as shown below.

   Pass the Talking Stick around the circle.

   A. Open circle: animal visualization (See Opening examples and Spirit Guide activity on page 37.)
   B. Purpose of this program: To discover our mentors and uncover our inner heroes.
   C. Listen to a story: Choose a hero story that suits your purpose, one that creates an introductory discussion opportunity. Recommendation: "Sir Gawain and the Green Knight" (see *Dancing at the Crossroads: Stories and Activities for At-Risk Youth Programs*.)
   D. Discuss what makes a hero. You may want to use chart paper to make a list of hero attributes. Remember to add the materials to your list.
   E. Receive the first quest.

   Suggestions:

   1. Becoming a dragon rider or dragon slayer. What do you feel you have to overcome to get where you want to be in life? What would that look like as a dragon?

      A. Decorate folders with the dragon to be tamed.
      B. Come to session two prepared to identify something you can do to overcome this obstacle.

   C. Set a "real" life challenge for the participants. For example, if they decide that they need to communicate better with others, challenge them to choose one person and make some gesture to that person. It could be something as simple as a smile or saying hello. Be careful not to make this first quest unobtainable. The key to success is for the goals to be in the realm of what is possible. Each session, the challenge could become more difficult.

2. Journal Activity: Some youth will not wish to participate in this activity. You will need to decide in advance, perhaps with the group, what to do in this situation. It may be best to allow those who do not want to write, to sit quietly while the others do it. You may need to eliminate the writing altogether. You could substitute group discussion. Journaling is very effective and you may also need to teach the youth some ways of journaling beforehand. The purpose of this activity is to have a thoughtful debriefing opportunity for the youth. Journaling does not need to entail more than one or two sentences.

   Suggestions:

   A. Animal visualization experience (see page 38)
   B. Ideas for the dragon quest
   C. Thoughts about the story told

3. Optional Art activity. If you are using the Green Belt activity (See Appendix VI). This can also be done as shown in Session Two.

4. Q & A and sharing.

5. Discuss next session. You may give a quest at this time or just explain what you plan to do with the youth.

6. Close the circle with some activity that can be consistently used. (See Closings examples. on page 41)

Session Two: A Hero's Timeline

This is an activity to help youth discover their own stories. The goal is to help them unfold their own past, look for weaknesses and strengths, with an emphasis on strengths, and act as a follow-up to the story chosen in session one.

Materials: talking stick, permanent markers, green belt materials (strips of green cloth or paper), timeline paper such as roll of adding machine paper, stickers and pencils, folders and handouts.

1. Open circle: Revisit animal guides (see page 37).

   Create a HeroQuest® talking stick with animal guides by allowing the youth to draw their animal guides on the stick with a marker.

2.. Review last session's story message. If you have not already begun making the green belts, begin now. If the youth are in a secure setting, they may need to turn in their belts before returning to their residence. This is to avoid self-injury. You may want to check with the facility in advance.

   Optional: If you chose a different story or follow up activity for the first session, you may want to use a different activity. Whatever you choose to use should be consistent with your plan for the final celebration. In this way, the youth see a progression toward their goal.

3. A story about a personal quest by the facilitator. This should be a personal experience story that emphasizes a positive way to overcome adversity.

4. Discuss what happens to the hero that sets them apart from others.

   A. Birth: The hero usually has an unusual birth or childhood.

   B. The hero's test: Something may happen to the hero that acts as a "wake up" and sets the process in motion.

   C. Calling: The hero may have a calling, such as a prophecy. They may or may not be aware of it.

5. Begin having each youth create a Hero's Timeline. They may add to these timelines anytime, so if any feel they cannot place everything on their timeline during this session, include time each session for additions.
   A. They should include their birth date and any unusual circumstances surrounding their birth. For example, maybe they were premature, twins, or a difficult birth.
   B. Tests, Challenges they had to overcome, or have yet to overcome.
   C. Prophecies made by others. For example: A teacher may have told them that they would do great things, or someone may have acknowledged some ability they have.
   D. Where they are now and anything important explaining how they got there.
   E. The end of their journey: A prediction at the end of their timeline showing their goals for adulthood.
6. Share belts and timelines.
7. Discussion about HeroQuest: participants share their experiences as Dragon Riders from Session One. Did they accomplish the quest? If so, award one bead, sticker, patch, or whatever you have decided to affix to their belts as proof of accomplishment. Announce that the youth are now Level One Dragon Riders. May give a new quest.
8. Optional Journaling: thoughts about heroes and what makes someone a hero. You may do an optional art activity if preferred.
9. Discuss following session.
10. Close circle (see page 41).

Session Three: Reflecting the Hero, Defining the Villain

Materials: talking stick, journals, folders, pens

1. Open circle (see page 37): Name the nemesis. Pass the talking stick and ask each youth to give their dragon a name.

2. Discuss the power of names and the way people in various cultures view that power. Example: In some cultures children's names are changed when they become an adult. In others, a secret name is given that is only known to the recipient and perhaps their mentor. Sometimes it is believed that the living should not speak the names of the dead. Knowing the name of that which we must overcome; our enemy, or fear, gives us power over it.

3. How does the nemesis serve the hero in many stories?

   In our hero stories, what purpose does the villain serve?

   Answer: They are the mirror images of the hero. By observing the nemesis, the villain is able to see what he or she could become. The same is true of the mentor. Examples: Luke Skywalker could have become like Darth Vader, or he could have become like Obi Wan, or Yoda.

4. The youth will hear a story by the presenter.

   Suggestion: "The Magic Tapestry," this story contrasts a hero against the villain. In this story, all the brothers have the same opportunities, but choose different paths. This choice makes or breaks the hero.

5. Journal: Nemesis names, thoughts about the story.

   A. Youth may write their nemesis name on their folder with the dragon drawings.

   B. Journaling helps them keep a record of the journey they are taking through this process.

6. Optional art activity and/or sharing of activities being completed. Include discussion of completed quests and awards. New quest if desired. You may use discussion of next session to give a quest. Allow time for

additions to timelines. Remember, the quests are personal challenges to help the youth meet their goals. Keep them small and obtainable

7. Discuss next session.
8. Close circle. (see page 41)

Session Four: Defining the Other Players

Materials: Talking stick, journals, folders, pens, chart paper, markers, and movie video.

1. Open circle (see page 37): Can the hero and the nemesis have anything in common?
2. Discuss Harry Potter and Star Wars. How were the heroes and villains created?

   Use *Star Wars: Revenge of the Sith* and *Harry Potter and the Goblet of Fire*. In these movies the hero is the same as the villain. In life, we are all one-step away from the darkness. We walk on the edge between light and the dark side. If we slip, we can be redeemed. However, the longer we spend in the darkness, the more we become like the villain.

3. Create a list of players:

   Hero

   Nemesis

   Mentor

   Tool(s) to move the story

   A. Object (spells, magic items, super powers, abilities)
   B. Person (a chance meeting)
   C. Event (i.e The bears wake Goldilocks.)

4. Create a scenario for the hero's birth and life purpose. This may be the beginning of a group story or individual stories written by the youth. It does not need to be an actual story. It could be a list of statements in their journal. Journal: Hero name, birth and purpose. Use timelines to create a story of your birth.

5. Share journal ideas and award dragon rider tokens for accomplished quests.
   A. Listen to a story that demonstrates the hero/nemesis relationship and the hero's purpose.
6. Begin to watch video. Videos are optional if time permits
7. Discuss next session.
8. Close circle (see page 41).

Session Five: The Hero's Mentor and Tools.

Materials: talking stick, journals, folders, pens, movie video/DVD.

1. Open circle (see page 37): What is meant by a set back? What happens in many stories to hold the hero back from the quest? Find an event on your timeline that could be considered a set back.
2. Journal a story about your timeline set back. (This can also be done verbally by passing the talking stick around the circle.).
3. Discuss what choices the hero makes during a set back.

   Discuss how the nemesis creates the set back and how the mentor helps the hero. Who or what helps us accomplish our goals? Define personal mentors and how they might help us overcome this dragon we are fighting.
4. Discuss set backs the hero faces and how they overcome those setbacks. Relate this to the youth's personal experience.
5. Give "Dragon Rider" awards.
6. If time permits, watch next section of the movie that shows the character's setbacks and results.
7. Write a statement on the front of your folder that explains the set back you must overcome to tame your dragon. Discuss how this realization serves the hero's success?
8. Optional: for programs longer than six session s you may begin a hero saga such as Hercules.

9. Discuss next session
10. Close circle (see page 41).

Session Six Celebration

This is the culmination of a six-session program. If longer programs are possible, the following curriculum additions may be made.

Your celebration should include the awarding of final dragon rider status to those who obtained it. If using the Green Belt activity, you may ask each youth to hand their belt to you as Sir Gawain did in the story. You then hand it back with some wish for their future.

Additional Sessions for HeroQuest® as needed.

Optional Session Six: The Battle

Materials: talking stick, journals, folders, pens, movie video/DVD

1. Open circle (see page 37): What kinds of battles do we have to fight, daily, yearly, lifelong? What tools help us fight our battles? Which ones work best?
2. Journal a story about one important battle on your timeline.
3. View a final battle between the hero and nemesis. Discuss what happened and the possible aftermaths.
4. Give "Dragon Rider" awards.
5. Role Play a battle scenario using a simple form of charades and choreographed movements. You may want to invite guest dancers to do this if the youth are not able due to behavior issues.
6. Listen to the part-two story of a hero saga.
7. Discuss next session.
8. Close circle (see page 41).

Optional Session Seven: The Aftermath and Final Chapter

Materials: talking stick, journals, folders, pens, movie video/DVD, collage materials including magazines, glue, scissors, poster board, other objects.

1. Open circle(see page 37): So, what happens to the hero once the journey is at an end? Do they have a new adventure? Do they retire? Does the hero become someone else's mentor? What else could they do?
2. Journal: What will your legacy be? How do you want to be remembered?
3. Watch movie conclusion.
4. Give "Dragon Rider" awards.
5. Divide into groups and create a collage triptych that shows the hero's journey. This artwork will reflect the beginning, middle, and end of the hero's journey.
6. Share triptychs.
7. Listen to part three of the hero saga.
8. Discuss who the youth think of as hero's in the international, national, and local communities. Who are the heroes in their personal communities? Are they friends, family, or social contacts? If they could choose one local hero they would like to meet, who would it be? What is the difference between a physical, mental, or spiritual hero? How are they alike?
9. Discuss next session.
10. Close circle (see page 41).

Optional Session Eight: The Hero's Weakness and Strength

Materials: talking stick, journals, folders, pens, index cards, simple props

1. Open circle (see page 37): What are the hero's greatest weaknesses and strengths?
2. Journal possible answers to the question above.

3. Listen to part four of the hero saga
4. Using index cards, create group Hercules (Hero cards) events cards based on individual journal and timeline stories. Be sure to change the names so the youth are not recognized. One pile will consist of helpers and tools, one of villains, and one of actual events.
5. Divide into groups.
6. Each group chooses an event card from each pile and decides how to portray that event in role-play.
7. Groups take turns acting out their scenes.
8. Discuss next session.
9. Close circle.

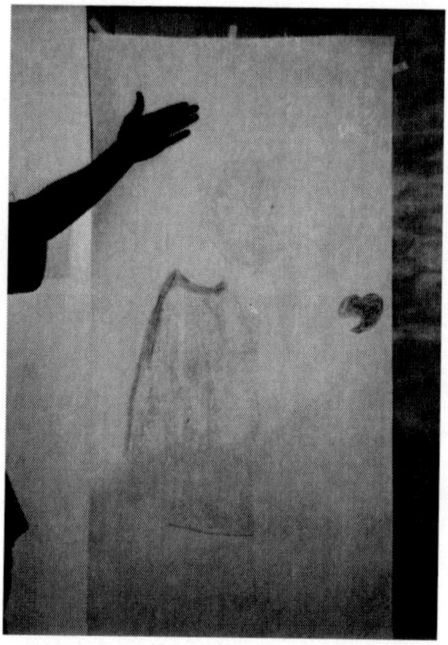

"Youth with a disconnected head, holds his heart in his hand. Love is his gift to the world."

Optional Week Nine: Creating a Personal Hero's Identity

Materials: talking stick, journals, folders, pens, life-size sheets of paper, sidewalk chalk or multicolored jumbo markers, chart paper, markers, masking tape, writing paper, envelopes, and stamps.

1. Open circle (see page 37): If you are the hero in the story, how do you look? What are your super powers? What gift do you offer to the world?
2. Journal possible answers to the question above.
3. Discuss what we would like our ideal world to look like. What needs to be left in? What needs to be removed?
4. Role play the destruction of those things we wish to remove. Suggestion: Throw things into an imaginary fire.

Divide into groups to trace an outline of each other. For some youth this may require adult supervision.

5. Each youth will use chalk or markers to color in the details of their super hero.
6. Listen to a hero story by the presenter.
7. Share our hero stories. Youth may tell their story, read their journal, or share their artwork hero.
8. Youths write a letter to themselves stating what they'd like to be doing in nine months.
9. Discuss next session.
10. Close circle (see page 41).

Optional Session Ten: Creating a Community Identity Circle

Materials: talking stick, journals, folders, pens, large sheets of paper, pencils, colored markers, chart paper, markers, and role-playing community cards.

1. Open circle: How does the butterfly effect relate to our immediate communities? Our outer-circle communities? Our world communities? "The Butterfly Effect" states that butterflies in South America create wind with their wings that affects the climate miles away. This idea can be applied to how one person's actions affect another.
2. Discuss the butter fly effect and how we are each part of the whole picture.
3. Journal personal reflections.
4. What are the inner and outer circles of communities? To what different communities do we belong?
5. Youth discuss these with partners.

6. Role play some different community relationships.
7. Each youth will draw and label their community circles on the large paper. This is the same as the mandala activity found on page 137.
8. Create a group hero story.
9. Discuss next session.
10. Close circle.

Optional Session Eleven: Listen to Group Hero Story and Celebrate the Hero's Journey.

Materials: talking stick, journals, folders, pens, group story, food, belts etc.

1. Open circle (seep page 37): Revisit our animal guides.
2. Journal animal guide experiences.
3. Listen to the group story.
4. Optional: performance of a final quest. This may be done as show and tell, spoken, read, or whatever you have decided to use with the group.
5. Hand out Dragon Rider awards.
6. Optional: a guest presenter or visiting hero from the community.
7. Initiation of the hero: Graduation from the program and ceremony of awards. Invite family, friends, and community if appropriate.
8. Close circle (see page 41).
9. Party snacks and a reception.

The following is a requirement sheet developed for a particular agency. The reader may find it helpful as a model for his or her own use.

Requirements for HeroQuest®

- *Enrollment*: maximum and minimums. Adult supervision?
- *Program Length*:
- *Session Length*:

How much will you charge?:

Will you need?

Clearance for recording or photographing youth.

Materials or funding for guests and food.

Rights and Proceeds

- *Documentation*: Camera, film, tape recorder, and cassettes, video camera, and tape.

  These will remain the property of __________. Copies of any recorded materials (photos, cassettes, youth written material) will be made available to _________ upon request.

- *Materials*: Who will own and who will distribute recorded materials? Who is responsible for what items?

Optional: Youth expectations.

- Youth will participate in setting rules for the group.
- Youth will participate in weekly activities and complete assignments to the best of their ability.
- Youth will assist in all aspects of decision-making for the group, particularly the selection of a guest hero and writing a group story.
- Youth will be prepared by bringing their pens, journals, and folders to each session along with any assignments. Youth will complete a pre and post evaluation.

Chapter 7
Conclusion

No one book can offer all the information available but I hope by sharing the many years worth of knowledge I have gathered has at least paved the road for you. If I can summarize very shortly what you will need to be successful, I would say:

Respect the young people with whom you will work no matter what their situation and remember, many have lost their childhoods. Our job is to give some of that back to them.

Our other job is to teach these young people the power of story so they are better equipped to navigate life now and later.

Be kind to yourself. You may see and hear horrible things. You need to remember not to take it personally. You are giving a gift that may not always be readily accepted. Remember why you are giving it and the rest will fall into place. Have a support system either within the facility where you are working or personally. Debriefing is valuable. Beware of vicarious trauma.

Please do not hesitate to contact the author with questions about these programs or ideas of your own. Together we can make a difference and build a better tomorrow, *One Child at a Time.*

Appendix

Appendix I

Archetypes

The following archetypes and symbols were taken from several sources shown in the bibliography of this book. In addition, some of the ideas presented are based on the author's experience and generally accepted themes in the storytelling community. It is important to note, while these ideas can form a foundation on which to build a story and activity session, listeners should be allowed to make their own interpretations. Only a few examples can be included in this book. The storyteller is encouraged to explore symbols in stories before telling the story. (See "Unlocking the Power of Story" Workshop on page 8)

BIRD: The messenger. Beautiful birds usually bring good news whereas the raven is the harbinger of evil tidings.

BLACK, WHITE, RED, GREEN, PURPLE: These are the color symbols most widely used. Black is void, the absence of spectral color, dark and dangerous. White is pure, holy, reverent, the color of wisdom, all spectral colors mixed together. Red is death and war. Green can be envy, but is usually associated with life. Purple is power. This idea of power may come from the fact that purple is an expensive color to make from natural sources. In the middle ages, it was reserved for royalty for this reason.

BUTTERFLY, SNAKE, PHOENIX: These symbols are transformative. The butterfly changes completely from caterpillar to something beautiful. It represents the hero's journey. On the other hand, the snake emerges from its old skin looking just as it did before. Where the butterfly is a completed journey, the snake reminds us that we can renew ourselves and start over again. Snakes are sometimes equated with sneakiness and evil. The Phoenix is destroyed in fire only to be born again. Renewal, rebirth, and opportunity for resurrection are the themes presented by these archetypes.

DARK and LIGHT: Sometimes shown as black and white, these elements are tied to the physical nature of day and night. We can see where we are going in the daytime. The most fearsome creatures of the world sleep during these hours. At night, those creatures prowl the earth and hunt for food. We cannot see the landscapes visible to us during the day. Therefore, darkness is feared. Light equals goodness, dark is dangerous and evil. One interesting twist on the idea of evil darkness is that it is also the time we sleep and rejuvenate. Without it, there can be no rebirth.

DRAGONS: These beasts have been portrayed as both good and evil depending on their origins. In Christianized story, they are dark and must be destroyed. In Oriental tradition, the dragon is elemental and revered. No matter how dragons are viewed, they are the embodiments of ageless wisdom both good and evil. They live long lives, acquire treasure, and have creative/destructive powers.

FOOL, JESTER, TRICKSTER: In Medieval history, the Fool or Jester played the role of more than just an entertainer. Their tricks and jokes remind us not to be too serious, for in our playfulness we find many answers. In addition, they are able to speak terrible truths through their tomfoolery that most people would shun if lectured outright. The fool and jester play very much the same role as story. They teach without us knowing it. Most often the fool is a sidekick to hero or king.

The trickster allows the characters to fail. He will laugh at them and perhaps anger them so the lessons learned are solid.

FOREST: The great unknown. Characters lose their way and meet many challenges in the forest.

HERO, WARRIOR, and CHILD: Often portrayed as male, but found as female in many stories, the hero is the young warrior or child searching for answers. They seldom choose the path before them. Instead, the hero is thrown into a situation that tests their limits and challenges their abilities. The hero needs a mentor, a tool, or super ability to succeed. The hero is on a journey toward adulthood and enlightenment.

Children are outwardly powerless and small, yet they defeat the giants and witches. They are good models for other young people. They are empowering figures who grow, if not physically. The child reminds us that in naivety there is courage and often wisdom. This wisdom comes from the same place as the wise man's wisdom. Children are not encumbered by their own experiences. They see the world and its puzzles from a different perspective than the adult. Sometimes we find both a boy and girl traveling together. This allows us to see both sides of self, the protector and the nurturer.

HOUSE: A place of security. As with evil parents, when the security of house and home get turned around, we are placed on alert that something is wrong and an adventure will take place. The house is supposed to be safe territory.

KING, QUEEN, and CLERGY: Rulers in story hold omnipotent power over life and death, but do not know all the answers. Sometimes they are foolish in their actions and may have forgotten humility. They offer the quest to someone else because they cannot journey beyond the high status they have already obtained.

MOTHER, FATHER: Mothers represent the nurturing spirit, the creator of life. She provides a look at inner wisdom. Her protection is emotional. The father is the provider of what is outside self. He is the one who protects physically. When these story characters do not live up to these expectations, such as the mother and father in Hansel and Gretel, we find them disturbing. Since the nemesis is the shadow-self, then wicked mothers or fathers are the shadows of the true beings who walk in the light and live up to our expectations.

NEMESIS: May take the form of giant, monster, witch, parent, stepparent, or natural elements. The purpose of the NEMESIS is to motivate the hero to grow beyond his or her limits. They represent the darker side of the hero, often having identical characteristics, the mirror image of the hero in the shadow world.

PATH, CIRCLE, SPIRAL, MAZE: The path is the journey a character must take, but sometimes they need to choose from many paths along the way. A circular path will take them back to their place of origin. In story, the circle reminds us that life is a continuing journey from birth to death to birth again. The circle, like the PHOENIX, offers hope for renewal.

A spiral, unlike the circle, will never take us back to the place we began. Instead, a spiral takes us ever toward the center of self and greater understanding of life's mysteries. However, as long as we keep moving in the spiral it is impossible to get lost. There is a definite beginning and an end.

The maze is a journey where we can easily become lost. We are assured there is a prize somewhere within it, but we must find it on our own. When characters enter the maze, they must rely on instinct and the teachings of their mentors. The teacher may not enter with the student. The maze is the master-test on the hero's journey.

RAINBOW: The rainbow foretells a promising future. In the Bible, God promised never to destroy mankind by flood again. The rainbow is His signature on that promise. The rainbow is hopeful.

SUN and MOON: In most cultures, the sun is male and the moon is female. There are cultures that view them the other way around. It is always advisable to explore this before telling a story.

Both the sun and the moon shed light upon the earth. However, the moon does not have its own light. Its light is borrowed from the sun. They may be man and wife, or brother and sister.

THREE, FOUR, SEVEN, NINE: Of these numbers, four is the least found. Life is divided in threes. The third is the tiebreaker. Without three, there would only be black and white, right and wrong, good and evil. No opportunity for free thought and movement would exist. The third is the gray zone. Three offers a different perception of directionality: Heaven, earth, hell or Earth, sea, sky.

Four is seen most often in the seasons and cardinal directions. The changing seasons are life's changes; childhood, adolescence, adulthood, and old age. When it comes to the directions, a character will choose but they are all on the same plane of existence. The earth has four corners. With the use of four, the character is earthbound. (Three is the only number that allows a character to move outside the mortal realm.)

Seven is the number of days in the week. Odd numbers always allow for a middle ground. Nine are the months of gestation for human birth. This makes nine a number of life and living. In story, we will find seven or nine children in a family. These numbers, as well as five, are typical numbers for animal litters.

TREASURE: While treasures are usually tangible, they actually represent what we cannot hold in our hands, such as newfound experience and wisdom.

UNICORNS: The unicorn is absolute purity. It has healing powers and can only be touched by the virgin.

VIRGIN: While this is associated with sexual experience, virginity in story is more about one who is not soiled in thought, word, or deed. Pure and untouched.

WATER: Represents cleansing and a gateway to the other world. Water separates places and times in stories. It acts as a transition for the characters. Beyond and beneath it are other spirits and lands. Water may be clear, mirror like, or murky. Each of these conditions lends a different feel to the nature of what lies beyond.

WISE HERMIT, SAGE, SEER, PROPHET, BEGGAR, OR TRAVELER: Often male and aged, these characters are the equivalent of the female witch and offer the same assistance to the story's main characters. Almost all witches and wise men live in hermitage conditions. This is an important element as it separates them from the "real" world and offers these teachers fewer distractions. In this way, they are able to meditate on the higher forces of life.

The beggar and traveler usually come to the story in disguise. They are there to give direction and to test the hero, often on a humanitarian level. Can warriors who are destructive keep their humanity? This is the beggar/traveler's purpose in story.

The seer or prophet is blind in most stories, which is an interesting contradiction. Their sight is not of this world. They are not distracted by the common life.

WITCH: There are witches in many different stories. They basically represent the same thing. They are typically older women who have much knowledge about magic and/or life in general. Their knowledge includes the workings of the earth, sea, and sky. They are familiar with animals and plants. Having gained negative status in the Christian world, witches are often viewed as evil. They are almost always ugly and cruel. They are helpers to the characters in story, offering advice, magical assistance, and motivation.

WOLF: In most European stories, Wolf is dark and evil. Many Native American stories see Wolf as a helper and powerful spirit. Wolf's reputation as a dark being may be due to his elusive nature and the fact that wolves may attack livestock, which is needed for human survival. In story, Wolf is a trickster who devours. The act of devouring can be equated with consuming the power and wisdom of another.

Appendix II

Archetypes Worksheet

Archetypes: people and animals that represent ideas such as

- wisdom = witch, wizard, old man or old woman
- strength = warrior
- compassion = young woman
- love = mother
- anger = monster

Metaphors: objects, colors and numbers that represent ideas such as

- security = house
- fear = night
- the unknown = forest
- anger = red
- strength = tower

A Story Needs a Main Character, a Plot, and a Resolution

- **MAIN CHARACTER NEEDS:**
  A nemeses, villain or something to overcome
- **PLOT NEEDS:**
  Basic background of what is or has happened
- **CLIMAX:**
  When the main character is in the most danger, receives help or discovers answer)
- **RESOLUTION NEEDS:**
  Main character uses new knowledge or power to solve the problem
- **THE END**

TELLING A STORY:
Everybody will tell a story differently.
It is a personal choice.

WRITING OR TELLING:
Everybody will use the tools that fit them best. You can write a draft copy and tell the whole story, write the story out completely, or make it up in your head from start to finish.

Developing Your Story

Some things to consider:

1 You are the main character in your story. You may choose to be an animal or a person. What archetype represents you best? (Start to use "She" instead of "I" or "me".

She is a ______________________________

2. What is the problem you are facing or did face that you want to use as your story problem? Can that problem be represented as an archetype or metaphor? What would it be?

____

____

3. What does your character have to go through or do to find the answer

She must ______________________________

____

4. Does someone or something help her find the answer? Who or what

____

____

5. How is the answer revealed to the main character? (Climax

____

6. What does the character do with the new information to solve the problem? (Resolution)

____

____

Try telling your story as a once upon a time story:
Once upon a time ... the end.

Appendix III

Youth Issues and Story List

This list includes general issues for many of today's youth between the ages of twelve and twenty-one. Listed with each issue are the problems associated with that issue and suggestions for stories that deal with the issue. A source for each story is also given. Stories included in *Dancing at the Crossroads: Stories and Activities for At-Risk Youth Programs* are labeled (included).

Abandonment

"Philamondre" from the *Magic Orange Tree* ("One my Darling" Wolkstein 1997): A mother ignores her fourth daughter, Philamondre. After her three beloved daughters are taken by a monster, the mother goes to seek them, leaving Philamondre to fend for herself. Philmondre is adopted by a queen and raised as her own but Philamondre comes face to face with her biological mother unexpectedly and must decide whether or not to forgive her.

"Hansel and Gretel" (*Dancing at the Crossroads: A Guide for Caregivers in At-Risk Youth Programming*): This is a coming of age story. Abandoned youth find solace in the idea that we can overcome an adversity and become whole through our courage.

Domestic Abuse

May include physical, emotional, mental, and financial abuse.

"Moth to the Flame" by Lorna MacDonald Czarnota (included): With the help of a mentor, a young abused wife is able to leave an abusive relationship. Becky loves her husband, although he hits her. As with many abused women, she wonders if she can change him and stay with him. One night she decides to leave, but still vacillates between self-preservation and her love for him. Mildred, the ticket-taker at the bus depot, uses a metaphor of moths that die in the fire to help Becky see that she must not keep jumping back into the destructive relationship with her husband.

In most forms of abuse, there is a sense of helplessness. This story shows the need for a support system and the importance of safety and self-preservation. Other stories with this message include "Mr. Fox," "Mary Culhane and the Deadman," and "Vasslisa." (All included.)

Anger and Violence

"The Tiger's Whisker" (included): A woman seeking her husband's love when he becomes angry discovers that patience is what she needs to use in order to gain his trust. She must bring a tiger's whisker to the wise man so he can make a potion to cure her husband. Every day, she gets closer to the tiger until she can take the whisker. When the woman gives it to the wise man, he throws it in the fire. He tells her that it is not the whisker that will cure her husband. The process of patience she used in getting it was the cure.

"The Secrets of Heaven or Hell" (included): A wise man sits in his teahouse. A Samurai Warrior breaks down his door and demands to know the difference between heaven and hell. He grows angrier when the wise man ignores him. The wise man finally replies in a soft gentle tone, "That is hell." Confounded by this reply, the Samurai sits peacefully. "That is heaven," says the wise man.

"Wolves in My Heart" (included): Native American tale about a boy who dreams that there are two wolves in his heart. One is anger and one is love. The boy has had problems dealing with his peers. He asks his father which one of the wolves will win. His father replies "The one you feed." This story follows along the theme of, "Kill them with kindness."

"The Two Warriors" by Dan Keding (included): In this story two warriors meet to fight, but as they rest through the night they tell stories of their families. They cannot fight the next morning as planned because they now know each other.

"Clam and Bird" a Chinese fable based on "The Mussel and the Snipe" found in *Peace Tales* by Margaret Read MacDonald (1992) (included): A mussel is sunning on the beach when a snipe swoops down and grabs it. The two are caught in a life or death struggle over who will eat the other. Eventually, because neither will concede to the other, a fisherman takes them both.

Bullying

"Clam and Bird" a Chinese fable based on "The Mussel and the Snipe" found in *Peace Tales* by Margaret Read MacDonald (1992) (included).

"Wolves in My Heart" (included)

"The Ugly Duckling" by Hans Christian Anderson.

Date Rape

"Little Red Rides with a Hood" by Lorna MacDonald Czarnota (included).

Desire/Self Esteem/Self-Image

"Mary Culhane and the Deadman" (included): This story is difficult. It's very dark, but sometimes that is what the teens need. Mary has a symbiotic relationship with the Deadman, but she loses her own will to make right choices. Fortunately, Mary can find her strength of spirit and correct her mistakes in the end. It is a story about relationship to self and not selling out for something trivial.

"Scar Face Girl" (also the *Rough Face Girl* by Rafe Martin): This is an Abanaki Cinderella story that has roots as a historical tale. A chief has two daughters. While he is away, the oldest daughter abuses her sister. She will not allow the younger girl to have beautiful clothes or beautiful hair. What is worse, she scars her sister's face, arms, and legs with coals from the fire. In the end, the younger daughter who is honest marries the Rainbow Warrior. He makes her beautiful again. In some versions of the story, he punishes the older sister by turning her into an aspen tree. His other name is Strong Wind and when Strong passes, the aspen trembles.

"Owl" is a Haitian story. *The Magic Orange Tree* (Wolkstein, 1997): Owl hides his face from the girl he loves because he thinks he is ugly. She uncovers it and he runs away. She would have loved him anyway, but he never knows. She marries someone else. This is a self-esteem story.

"Vassalisa" (included): The girl protagonist never loses her sense of self even when abused by her caregivers. A Russian Cinderella tale and a hero's journey or coming-of-age story.

"The Youth and his Eagle," *Family of Earth & Sky* (1994) (included): This story speaks to risk-taking behaviors and how we are sometimes so in love with an idea that is not good for us. It highlights the consequences of letting go of important things, including those who truly love us. In this story, young people will find unconditional love, abandonment, trust breaking, risk-taking, enabling, co-dependency, hope and consequences for actions.

The Black Prince (*Dancing at the Crossroads: A Guide for Caregivers in At-Risk Youth Programming.*) A poor boy discovers that the girl he has fallen in love with is a princess. He believes she cannot love him as he is, so he seeks a magician who changes him into what he feels the princess will love. He finds out that she loved him the way he was when he was but a poor boy, but now it is too late to return to his old self

Eating Disorders

"Hansel and Gretel" (*Dancing at the Crossroads: A Guide for Caregivers in At-Risk Youth Programming*): The children in this classic tale are deprived of more than food. Later, when opportunity presents itself, the children become gluttons for what they need.

Many eating disorders have nothing to do with food deprivation.

Eating too much or too little is a tool for dealing with other problems. As with many behaviors, eating or not eating serves a purpose. The goals are to replace a negative behavior with a positive one, find and treat the root of the problem.

Hansel and Gretel grow through their suffering. They discover that food will not solve their deeper problems.

Forgiveness

"Philamondre" from the *Magic Orange Tree* ("One my Darling" Wolkstein 1997)

Husband and Wife/Friends/Parent-Child

"Star Woman's Basket" is an adaptation of "Black and White Cows," by Laura Simms *Ready-to-Tell Tales* by Holt and Mooney and found on an audio recording by Laura Simms, *Making Peace*, Earwig Recordings, Chicago. This story is about the trust between a husband and wife, and the betrayal of that trust. It strengthens the idea that trust is essential in a relationship, something most at-risk youth know and cherish.

"Sir Gawain and Dame Ragnell" (included): A story about judging "a book by its cover" and about keeping ones word of honor. It is a story about appearances and respect. This is also a story about self-empowerment through choice.

"The Blossom Tree," *Family of Earth & Sky*. 1994: The power of friendship and respectfulness for nature. The king wishes to cut down a beloved tree to make his house stronger, but the tree is saved by its friend.

"Philamondre" from the *Magic Orange Tree* ("One my Darling," Wolkstein 1997): a Cinderella story where a young girl is one of four daughters, but is not loved by her mother. Eventually the mother is in need of her daughter and the girl forgives her.

"Bleeding Heart" by Lorna MacDonald Czarnota, *Dancing at the Crossroads: A Guide for Caregivers in At-Risk Youth Programming*: A story for understanding unconditional love. An expectant mother receives words of wisdom from her mother-in-law regarding how to love her child, even during the most difficult times.

"The Empty Cage" by Lorna MacDonald Czarnota (included): A story of letting go and unselfish love. A woman who adopts three baby birds learns to let go of them as they grow apart from her, while at the same time realizing she will always love them and always be their mother.

"The Selkie" a Scottish folktale adapted by Lorna MacDonald Czarnota (included): A story of unselfish love and the need to maintain identity within a relationship. A man captures a mythical Selkie, but she is always torn between his world and hers. Eventually she must leave him in order to feel whole and healthy.

"Dancing in Dark Waters" an adaptation of Skeleton Woman, an Inuit tale (included). This story is about how compassion can make us whole again. This may be a compassion one gives to self or receives from others. A fisherman catches the skeleton and is afraid as she seemingly chases him home. Once he has a chance to see her condition, he takes pity on her. As he sleeps, she drinks his tears and sings herself back into existence. She stays with him and they are one.

Incarceration

"Hansel and Gretel" (*Dancing at the Crossroads: A Guide for Caregivers in At-Risk Youth Programming*)

"Mary Culhane and the Deadman" (included)

"The Red Shoes" by Hans Christian Anderson

Loss and Grief

"The Weeping Lass" (included): "The Weeping Lass at the Dancing Place" is from *Twelve Black Cats* by Sorche Nic Leods (see bibliography) A girl who cannot find happiness learns to let go of her grief when she is confronted by her dead love. She will not let him go, so he tries to take her to his grave. He tells her "No longer will you wet me with your tears. No longer will you keep me awake with your crying." She struggles to get free. Finally, she comes to realize that she must let him go and move on with her life.

Man-Woman/ Perpetrator-Victim

"Mr. Fox"(included): Mr. Fox is an abuser. The woman in the story is taken in by his looks, wealth, and power. Girls hearing this story will be taken in too and often comment on how they would like to have a man like Mr. Fox. Once they hear what he does, they change their minds. They understand the heroine's trouble and hope for her safety. This story is a cautionary tale about accepting things without questioning and looking for truth.

She does get away by her own wit and her brothers punish Mr. Fox. The brothers represent the positive male influences and reinforce the fact that family is a good safety net sometimes.

Mr. Fox represents deceit. Through questioning his truths, the heroine in the story avoids his lies and her own destruction.

Pregnancy and Parenthood

"Rapunzel" (*Dancing at the Crossroads: A Guide for Caregivers in At-Risk Youth Programming*): This is a coming-of-age story showing the birth of a child as a result of forbidden sexual activity. It can be a cautionary tale about taboo. The story ends with the mother, Rapunzel reuniting with the father, the prince. This story could also be used to start a discussion on the importance of the role of father and mother in a child's life.

"Rumpelstiltskin" (Brothers Grimm): A mother fights for custody of her child. This story has many layers and could be told from several points of view. The young woman, who later becomes a mother, must grow in the story to the point where her child is more important than her own life. While Rumpelstiltskin is not the child's father, she must outwit him to keep her child. Actual mention of the child's father is not seen in this story, so the story cannot be used as a "family" tale.

Relationships

Many youth we have been discussing come from families that have relationship problems. Whether it is a divorce, abuse, or death, their sense of relationship is already damaged in some way. Statistics show that these histories will repeat themselves in the child's relationship structures later in life.

The youth may be having problems with their immediate family relationships. These issues sometimes manifest later in their own marriages and parent/child situations.

Some stories model the "ideal" family, but the more powerful stories model youth experiences and show consequences of actions. It is not so simple as to say that listening to a story can change the path of a youth. Some may need therapeutic counseling. However, story is a powerful tool to implant ideas into the subconscious of the youth. Story recollection can serve them in time of need.

Responsibility

"Hansel and Gretel" (*Dancing at the Crossroads: A Guide for Caregivers in At-Risk Youth Programming*)

"The Magic Tapestry" (included)

"Sir Gawain and the Green Knight" (included)

Sexuality

"Little Red Riding Hood." Metaphor of a girl coming into her menses. (Grimms Brothers.)

Siblings

"Hansel and Gretel" (*Dancing at the Crossroads: A Guide for Caregivers in At-Risk Youth Programming*): A story of roles and cooperation.

Substance Abuse

"Monk and the Moon" based on "Giving the Moon," *Wisdom Tales From Around the World*, Heather Forest (1996). Addicts will often only know the experience that drugs give them. This story reminds us that the things of real value in life may be lost to one who is on a drug high or intoxicated.

"The Red Shoes" by Hans Christian Anderson.

"Mary Culhane and the Deadman" (included)]

"The Boy Who Thought He was a Man" (included). A boy does what he knows might possibly harm him, because the snake tells him he will feel good if he does.]

Storyteller, Elizabeth Ellis tells a simple parable about addiction. "There was a man who died. He was given the choice between heaven and hell. He chose hell because he knew the names of the streets."

Suicide

"Footprints in the Snow" by Lorna MacDonald Czarnota (included): While originally intended as a story about a spiritual rebirth, this story can address the issue of suicide. The story is about finding a new beginning in an old situation through a metaphorical death and rebirth.

Teachers

"Monk and the Moon" based on "Giving the Moon," *Wisdom Tales From Around the World*, Heather Forest (1996): A wise man watches the moon with admiration for its beauty. He is a poor man with only a small hut and the clothes on his back. As he sits, he sees a robber sneaking up the hillside. The robber tears the old man's house apart while searching for something of value. He confronts the old man and demands his clothes. The wise man gives them and the robber, thinking he has taken the old man's only things of value, is satisfied and leaves. "If he had asked," says the wise man to the listener. "I would have given him the moon." This story shows that what is valued most is not always tangible. There are people who will show us, if we remain patient and open to the lesson.

"Spider's Dance" by Lorna Czarnota, *Dancing in Dark Waters*, CD: This story highlights the role of a teacher and the importance of passing knowledge to the student. A harper who has kept her knowledge private is on her deathbed when she realizes her knowledge will die with her. In one last wish, she asks for a student. She is transformed into a spider that teaches a young man, who never took the time to learn the harp from his father.

"Boy Who Hid in the King's Heart" is an adaptation of a Turkish tale by Laura Simms. ("The Boy Who Hid in the King's Heart," *Parabola Magazine*: Issue on SOUL.) A king seeks a teacher and is presented with a mere boy. He tests the boy, but the boy grows weary of the rigorous questions and asks to play a game. They play hide and seek. The boy quickly finds the king, but the king cannot find the boy when it is his turn. The boy is hidden in the king's heart. He teaches the king that the heart is the place where what we seek lies hidden.

"Moth to the Flame" by Lorna MacDonald Czarnota (included). This story is a good example of archetypal mentors as wise women who guide through example. "Moth to the Flame" is a story about an abused woman.

"Djuha's Sleeve," *Favorite Folktales from Around the World*. Jane Yolan (1986): Djuha is a wise man that figures prominently in several stories from the Middle East. All Djuha stories are teaching stories. In this story, Djuha teaches the old adage "You can't tell a book by its cover." Dressed in rags, Djuha visits a friend's house and is refused entry. When he changes into his good clothes, he is admitted and given respect. Djuha does not respond to the compliment, instead he compliments his sleeve, after all that is what they respected, not him.

Transition, Transformation, Coming of Age

"Nastai" (included): a Saami tale about a young girl who finds her own wisdom using that of her mother.

"Philamondre" from the *Magic Orange Tree* ("One my Darling," Wolkstein 1997)

"Vassalisa" (included)

"Hansel and Gretel" (*Dancing at the Crossroads: A Guide for Caregivers in At-Risk Youth Programming*)

"Sir Gawain and the Green Knight" (included)

Appendix IV

Examples of Questionnaires and Personal Survey Tools

Pre-Evaluation Empowerment Through Story

Expectations Rating: Please read each statement and circle whether you: SA) strongly agree, (A) agree, (D) disagree, or (SD) strongly disagree.

Do not put your name on this sheet.

1. I will be given a chance to help others.
   SA A D SD
2. I will be able to help plan and share my ideas.
   SA A D SD
3. The adults in this program will care about me.
   SA A D SD
4. The adults will listen to what I have to say.
   SA A D SD
5. I will feel like I belong.
   SA A D SD
6. I will feel important.
   SA A D SD
7. I will want to do well in school.
   SA A D SD
8. I will be challenged to do my best.
   SA A D SD
9. I will want to learn about new things.
   SA A D SD
10. I will learn about what is okay to do and what is not.
    SA A D SD
11. I will want to try harder in school.
    SA A D SD
12. I will make better decisions.
    SA A D SD

13. I will realize I have a lot to be proud of.
    SA A D SD
14. I will get along with others.
    SA A D SD
15. I will learn I can do things I never thought I could.
    SA A D SD
16. I will make and keep friends.
    SA A D SD
17. I will feel successful.
    SA A D SD
18. I will learn to respect others and their ideas.
    SA A D SD
19. I will learn to care more for other people.
    SA A D SD
20. Being responsible will be important to me.
    SA A D SD

Post Pre-Evaluation Empowerment Through Story

Expectations Rating: Please read each statement and circle whether you: SA) strongly agree, (A) agree, (D) disagree, or (SD) strongly disagree.

Do not put your name on this sheet.

1. What I have to say matters.
   SA A D SD
2. Other people listen to me.
   SA A D SD
3. I have a lot to offer the community.
   SA A D SD
4. I can find positive ways to express myself.
   SA A D SD
5. I feel like I belong.
   SA A D SD
6. I feel important.
   SA A D SD
7. I can set positive goals for myself.
   SA A D SD
8. I want to be challenged to do my best.
   SA A D SD
9. I want to learn about new things.
   SA A D SD
10. I listen while other people share their ideas.
    SA A D SD
11. I care about myself.
    SA A D SD
12. I make good decisions.
    SA A D SD
13. I respect others and their ideas.
    SA A D SD

14. I care about other people.
    SA A D SD
15. I realize I have a lot to be proud of.
    SA A D SD
16. I know I can do difficult things.
    SA A D SD
17. I feel successful.
    SA A D SD
18. Being responsible is important to me.
    SA A D SD
19. I solve conflicts in a positive way.
    SA A D SD
20. I have control over what happens to me.
    SA A D SD

Appendix V

Materials Resource List

This is a listing with contact informational for materials used in various suggested activities and gifting.

VOTIVE CANDLES: I purchase mine in bulk from a religious supply company. They come in individual plastic cups, which can be written on, in permanent marker. The brand I order is shipped from the Muench-Kreuzer Candle Company in Syracuse New York. They are called Disposable Votive Candles.

LED LIGHTS: Battery Operated Candles.net
http://www.batteryoperatedcandles.net/CG10280-CH-p-tea-lights.html
Nasco Arts and Crafts 1-800-558-9595 or www.info.nascofa.com
Sax Arts and Crafts 1-800-558-6696 or www.saxarts.com

FIMO CLAY: This is pliable clay once you have warmed it up with your hands. It comes in a variety of colors and when baked at approximately 350 degrees for about 15 minutes will become permanently hardened. It is perfect clay for bead making. Fimo clay may be purchased at most art supply stores.

MASK FORMS: These are available in a variety of styles but I like the whole mask best. You can also purchase a few items for decorating masks. Also consider flea markets and yard sales as a good source for decorations. Mask forms are white and you may want to spray paint a few in various colors before a session. We have painted them at the session but they take too long to dry.

COLORED SAND: You will need to purchase a large quantity of the sand. Begin collecting jars in which to keep it. Jars are easier to use than the little plastic bags the sand is shipped in.

Popsicle or craft sticks: Many arts supply companies will sell these by the box.

Faux Eagle feathers: Any kind of natural feather will work.
http://www.crazycrow.com/turkey-wing-feathers.
Colorful feathers are best for some projects such as mask-making. You can usually find bags of feathers at your local craft store.

Giant Rider-Waite Tarot Deck: a wonderful tarot card for exercises in metaphors and archetypes. You may need to modify the cards for some agencies.
U.S. Games Systems, Inc.
Stamford CT 06902

Gemstones, bracelets, tribal stones, and geodes: You will need to buy a large quantity of these products but they will last a long time.
GeoCentral 1-800-231-6083 or www.geocentralonline.com

Oriental Trading Company 1-800-228-2269 or www.orientaltrading.com
Trinkets of all kinds, including small bags of trouble dolls.

Glow-in-the-dark pebbles: A 1 pound bag contains just over 100 pebbles. Their 1" pebble white, glows blue. They also have blue/blue and green/green. About $20 per pound. You can also use ordinary white pebbles found at your local garden supply store.
CORE SYSTEMS P.O. Box 1545, Comox, BC Canada V9M 8A2
Toll-Free 1.855.777.2673 (CORE) or http://www.coregravel.ca/shop/

Appendix VI

Activities List with Materials

BASIC KIT: These are items you should carry all the time: Canvas Bag, snub-nose scissors, colored yarn, pens, blank paper.

MASK MAKING: Pre-painted blank mask forms, glue, glitter, pointed scissors. Only use sharp or pointed scissors under supervision. Other materials include snub-nose scissors, sequins, feathers, odd bits of yarn and ribbon, various types of macaroni, assorted beads, old mismatched earrings, old necklace chains, moss, seashells, natural materials such as pinecones, seeds and fern leaves etc., bits of felt and leather, assorted buttons, colored markers, pencils, paper plates and Styrofoam bowls.

Lay all the materials out by placing loose items on plates and in bowls. Only put out as many mask forms as you need for the group or they will be tempted to do more than one every time they make a mistake. Use mismatched earrings and odd chains, as youth will take them for wearing rather than for mask making. Of course it is okay to allow this, but you will go through a lot of supplies that way.

Note: an alternative is to have the youth decorate the inside of the mask as their real face, the outside as the face they show others.

HAND MIRROR: This idea first came to me when I stayed at a bed and breakfast. There was a silver hand-mirror turned over on the dresser in my room. I was compelled to look into it, then thought, "What if the face looking back at me is the face of the last person who looked in it." The idea of seeing the last person rather than myself, made me think about the issue of empathy toward others. I purchased a silver mirror at an antique dealer for about $20.

The youth seem to like the fact that they get to handle a very elaborate looking mirror. You could substitute a cheap plastic mirror if budget is a consideration.

PASS THE HAND MIRROR. Ask each person to look in it and describe something positive that the last viewer has to offer the group, the community, or society. This is a good activity for positive peer interaction and builds self-esteem for the individual being described. Use in conjunction with the story of "The Black Prince" to begin a writing activity or as a stand-alone activity. This activity can also be used with one youth, versus a group.

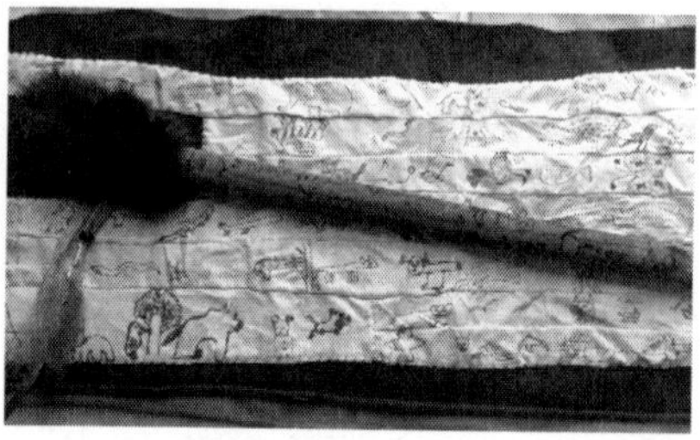

Talking Stick: Cover a 1" diameter wooden dowel with colored suede leather. Wrap one end with a scrap of fur and hang a feather from it. The back end should have streamers of suede and cloth. You will need permanent thin black markers for having the youth draw on the stick.

Fimo Medallions and Beads: Fimo clay, aluminum foil, toothpicks, cookie sheet, oven, and string.

Preheat the oven to 350° F. Give each youth an aluminum foil placemat on which to work to avoid clay sticking to work surface. Only give each youth a small amount of clay and let them share colors around. Otherwise, you end up with a lot of waste.

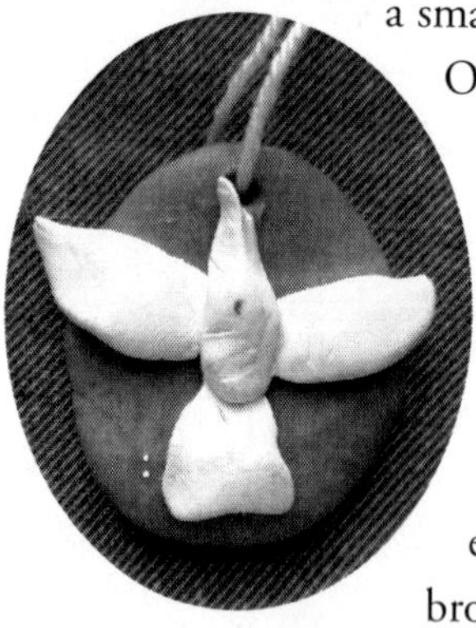

For Medallions: Make a circle of clay approximately 1 ½" in diameter. Apply any design in a contrasting color by gently pressing it into the background circle. Use a toothpick to make a hole for the string at the top of the medallion. Place medallions on cookie sheet. Bake for about 15 minutes. Check every so often to make sure they are not turning brown at the edges.

For Beads: To create colored beads, apply additional colors and shapes by gently pressing clay designs together. Pierce with a toothpick through the center for your string. Make sure it is a loose fit. Keep the toothpick in place when baking. Use same baking instructions as shown for medallions above.

CAUTION: The clay will be hot and may be slightly soft when it comes from the oven. It will need to cool and will harden further as it cools. Once cool, remove toothpicks. Place medallion or bead on a string long enough to fit over the youth's head. Use easy to break string in settings where suicide is an issue.

SAND-PAINTED MANDALAS: Heavy cardboard that is stiff enough not to bend, white glue, colored sand, water cups, small paint brushes, pencils with erasers, newspaper.

Youth draw mandala designs on cardboard. Spread newspaper on work surface. Mix white glue with a little water in the water cup. Trace drawing a little at a time with wet glue using paintbrush. Sprinkle colored sand on glue traced section. You can use the glue right from the bottle, but it runs thick and takes a long time to dry. Pour left over mixed color sand into a separate container and keep for future projects.

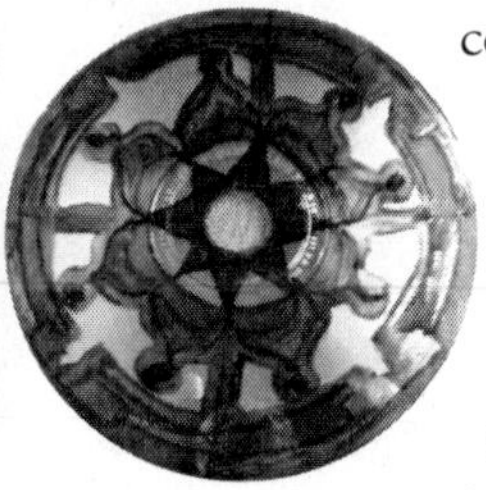

COMPACT-DISK MANDALAS: Compact disks and permanent colored markers. Youth draw designs on the readable side of the CDs. Save free and old used compact disks. You can also find blanks on sale from time to time. These can be hung with string in windows, on car mirrors, etc.

FRIENDSHIP TREE (SOS): Ceramic or plastic flower pot, moss or gravel, plaster mix, tree branch sprayed gold, strips of paper or cardboard 1 ½" x 3", ornament hangers, markers. Prepare in advance: Mix plaster and place gold painted tree branch into the plaster. Cover with moss or gravel. Give each youth a strip of paper and marker. Ask them to leave a message of hope for someone who will come to the tree in the future. Hang these on the friendship tree.

YARNS: Use pieces of yarn to represent our stories as an opening. Each person in the circle speaks or tells their story while tying their yarn onto the group ball of yarn. Holding the ball of yarn while speaking creates a stage for that individual to speak. Teens are often surprised by how large the ball of stories grows. This activity helps them feel that they are part of something larger than themselves.

SHADOW BOX: Create a shadow box collage of your desires for yourself. Materials: You will need a shoe box, cut up paper and cloth items, words

of various sizes, shapes, and colors, glue, scissors, coloring pens, crayons or paints, odds and ends such as small mirrors, glitter, and sequins. Youth may decorate the outside of the box differently than the inside. For instance, the outside can be their world now where the inside will represent their dream world. This can also be similar to the mask activity. Inside is the face we hide, outside is the face we show. You may substitute small square cardboard jewelry boxes with lids or breath mint boxes.

WISH BOXES: Remove labels and clean plastic non-dairy creamer containers. Decorate the exteriors with designs to represent self. Write wishes for the future on popsicle/craft sticks and place them in the box. Keep a few blanks available for future wishes, or write the wishes on folded pieces of paper instead. Materials: Plastic non-dairy creamer containers with lids, Popsicle sticks, slips of blank paper, thin permanent markers, colored waterproof markers.

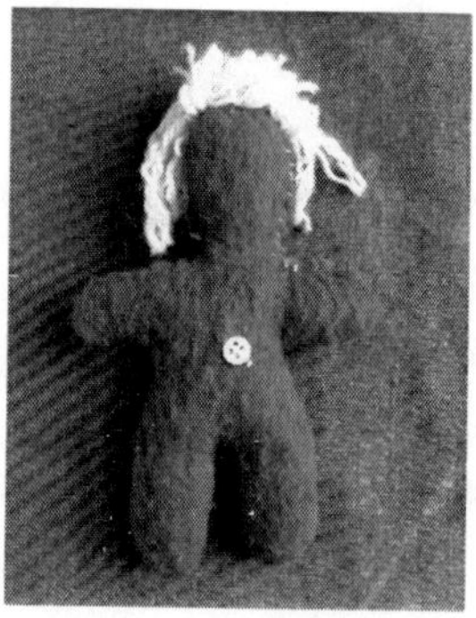

TROUBLE DOLLS: Felt or blanket cloth, large eyed needles, needle threaders, snub-nose scissors, thread, small buttons, yarn for hair, cotton batting for stuffing.

Precut the doll forms. Let the youth sew and finish as desired. You may have to help some of them with their sewing. This can be a frustrating and rewarding activity.

PERSONAL TAROT CARD DESIGN: Giant Rider-Waite Deck, colored markers, pencils, rulers, and poster board.

Some agencies may be leery of tarot cards, in which case an alternative is necessary. The

This youth's story begins "Once there was an invisible girl..." The cat in her garden of flowers is camouflaged

goal is for the teens to begin looking at illustrations as a set of metaphors. Have them choose three things they see in the card without thinking about it too much. What do they think these three things might represent? They should now design their own card representing who they are by using these three things in some form. Have the youth tell their story.

GREEN BELTS: The green belt can be used for initiation ceremonies and may accompany the story of "Sir Gawain and the Green Knight." The belts may be made of paper, cloth, or leather depending on funds and desired durability. In some situations, anything that can be used by teens to hang themselves or harm others might be confiscated. Paper will work in these instances. Always check with the facility. Stickers, beads, or other items may be attached to the belts. Materials will depend on which type of belt you choose to make. Stickers will not adhere to all materials. You may or may not have time to sew beads to the belts. You may want to invest in a tool that will allow you to affix gemstones and other craft items directly through the cloth. Investigate what is available at your local craft store. As with strung beads and medallions, if suicide is an issue, the belts should be able to tear apart.

TIMELINES: Create individual timelines to show important events and people in your life. Materials: roll of adding machine paper, which may be purchased at most office supply stores. Markers, pencils, stickers, scissors. Stickers may used by youth who may find it difficult to express feelings about specific timeline events. In addition, the stickers can be used to highlight significant events.

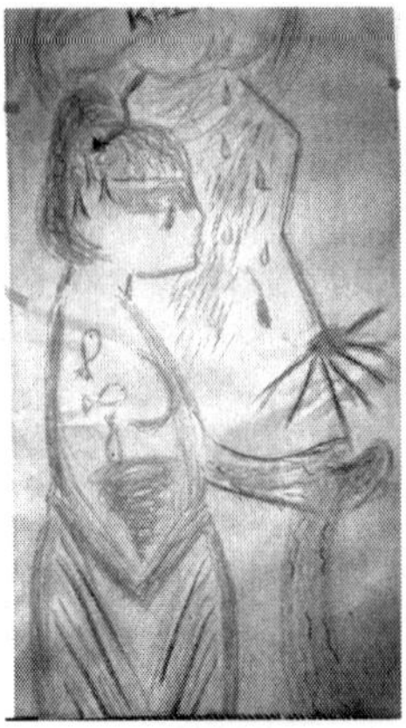

DESTROYING AND RECREATING THE WORLD: In this activity, the youth are told that they can have superhuman ability, be gods and goddesses, or creators of the world. You may combine this with the mask-making activity. They can create their godlike face. The facilitator asks the youth how they would use their new ability to change the world.

"There is no birth without death. We may each remove one things from the earth and destroy it by burning it in our imaginary fire." The youths are instructed to take something out of the world and throw it into the fire. "Now we may use our ability to add something of value back into the world, hopefully to make it a better place." Youths may draw pictures or just say what they would add. "There is no birth without death. You have it within yourselves to create yourselves new just as we did the world in this activity. What will you give up to make it happen?"

Ice Breakers:

PEACOCK FEATHER ROLE-PLAYING: This activity comes from storyteller, Ed Stivender. Using peacock feathers, have the youths do one or more of the following. Balance the feathers on the nose or palm. Use the feathers as props for various scenarios. For example, row a boat, shoot a bow, or sweep a floor. This may be done independently or in groups of two or three. Peacock feathers may also be given as tokens. For a peacock feather source see GeoCentral in the Appendix V.

DRUM NAMES: Using a drum have each youth beat out the rhythm in their names. Drums can be homemade or you may purchase lightweight inexpensive Middle Eastern or African drums. You only need one drum for this activity.

HAND SHAKE / EYE CONTACT NAMES: This is a very effective activity. Greet each youth by looking into their eyes and shaking their hand as you say their names. They then say your name in the same way. This is done three times as follows: Facilitator's name (Susan), Youth's name (Jake). Jake. Susan. Jake. Susan. Jake. Susan. The eye contact and sustained positive physical contact is what makes this powerful. Do not rush.

PUZZLE PIECES: Youth create a puzzle that represents whatever lesson you assign them. For instance, they can draw symbols using colors that represent themselves. One activity is for the session leader to create a "love piece" by drawing a heart on one of the puzzle pieces. Remove this piece before giving the blank puzzles to the youth to decorate. Ask them to create a puzzle that represents their lives and that they have a piece missing. You have that piece and it will be your gift to them. This is a good activity to use after "Dancing in Dark Waters (Skeleton Woman)". It symbolizes compassion.

Blank puzzles (Compoz-A-Puzzle) may be purchased from Sax Arts and Crafts. Sax Arts and Crafts 1-800-558-6696 or www.saxarts.com

Appendix VII

Hansel and Gretel: The Full Experimental Conversation

The following is an experimental role-play between Hansel and Gretel, played by the author, and their therapist, played by collaborator and social worker Diana Koch. The conversation was recorded on a cassette player and later transcribed. Some sections of the recording were unclear. Those are represented in the role-play with an "*". Any conversation or comments made by the actors, outside the role-play are noted.

In an actual therapeutic setting this might be only session one of many, or this sample session might be broken into two or more. This is completely dependant on the client's needs.

Therapist: Hi Hansel and Gretel. I'm Miss Diana and I'm the person you'll be talking to. Where would you like to sit? You can pick a place where you're close enough to talk to each other.

The children look around Miss Diana's office and realize they have never had furniture like that of her sofa and chairs. They didn't want to sit at the table but loved the sofa and chairs.

Therapist: Okay well, let's go sit there and get comfortable.

Everybody finds a seat. Gretel sits closest to the therapist.

Therapist: I'm so glad you came today, Hansel and Gretel. Like I said, my name is Miss Diana and my job is really to listen to kids when they had an experience that * I thought today we could spend a little time and you could just tell me what happened. * Is there something that you can share with me?

Storyteller: Wow, that feels like a really big thing.

Therapist: If I sensed that feeling in the children, we might play a game or something as an icebreaker.

Gretel:	Well, you know our mother really sucks.
Therapist:	Gretel, you think your mom really sucks?
Gretel:	Yeah.
Therapist:	What's that about?
Gretel:	Um. My dad sucks too.
Therapist:	So you're having some problems getting along?
Gretel:	Well, uh, yeah. They don't want us around. We went away and we came back. We're there. Well, uh, you know. They took us into the woods and they left us there.
Therapist:	They left you in the woods? That sounds pretty scary.
Gretel:	We didn't have much...
Hansel: interrupts	They don't want us there. They took us in the woods. They left us in the woods. They, they didn't leave us much food to eat. They said they'd be back and they…they lied. They didn't come back.
Therapist:	And Hansel, you were with Gretel when this happened?
Hansel:	Yeah. Um. I was pretty brave though.
Therapist:	Pretty brave. What did you do that you knew was brave?
Hansel:	Well, I didn't cry. She cried.
Gretel:	What do you expect?!
Therapist:	So Gretel, you cried and Hansel you didn't cry?
Hansel:	Nope.
Therapist:	You went through the same thing but you both looked at it differently. Which one of you could tell me a little more about what happened in the woods? You said your parents took in the woods and left you there. Can we take more of a look at that?

Hansel: Well they decided they couldn't afford to h-have us around anymore.

Therapist: Did they tell you that was the reason?

Hansel: They, they were talking about it.

Therapist: So you heard your parents talking?

Hansel: Next morning sh…she kicked the bed. She said get up and she gave us this stupid dried out old bread and...

Therapist: That doesn't sound very good.

Hansel: And they took us into the forest to chop wood and...

I dropped some stones on the ground and we followed those back home, but that was late at night.

Therapist: So Hansel, you heard your parents say that to you. Gretel, did you hear your parents say that or was it just you Hansel?

Hansel: Ah, we both heard 'em.

Therapist: You both heard them. Then the next day your mom got you up pretty rough. She kicked you out of bed and said let's get going. Sounds like you didn't have a very good breakfast. It didn't taste very good? It didn't feel like enough? Is that it?

Gretel: Yeah.

Therapist: And then your parents took you in the woods. Hansel, were you putting down stones even before you left? Were you doing that right away?

Hansel: Yeah, we didn't go very far. Um, I don't know why I had the idea when I heard my parents talking, but I saw the moon and it was shining on the stones, and I thought maybe they were like little light bulbs or something so I took them.

Therapist: Hm, little lights for you.

Hansel: Yahha.

Therapist: Yeah. So for whatever reason, maybe just it was interesting to do or fun to do or maybe some other reason, you felt you should leave a little path?

Hansel: Yeah. I didn't really (hesitation by Hansel) trust them?

Therapist: Were you thinking maybe something bad would happen?

Hansel: Well, they didn't want us around anymore and the whole family doesn't usually go to chop wood.

Therapist: So that was something out of the ordinary. Who usually went? Your dad?

Hansel: Yeah.

Therapist: So this was different than normal? And what was that like, just to know that something different was happening?

Hansel: Scary.

Therapist: So you thought about what happened the night before and now you were getting up really rough * You were worried. I think you were worried about it. What happened then?

Hansel: We went in the woods and it was getting dark. We sat down and, you know, our mom told us to eat our bread. They said they'd be back. We fell asleep and we woke up, but they weren't back. We saw the stones on the ground.

Therapist: So the stones were still there. How did that feel to see the stones there?

Hansel: That was good. I did the right thing.

Therapist: You knew you did the right thing. You marked the path.

Gretel:	Yeah, yeah, he's kind of smart sometimes.
Therapist:	(chuckles and says) Gretel, he's kind of smart sometimes. So what happened next?
Gretel:	Um, well he said we should follow them and we didn't have any other choice really.
Therapist:	And Gretel, how were you feeling that it was dark outside and the moon was shining on the stones?
Gretel:	I was really, I was really...
Hansel:	She cried. But I took care of her and, and…
Gretel:	What was I supposed to do? There was nothing else I could do but cry. I was scared.
Therapist:	It sounds pretty scary. Sometimes we all act a little differently...
Gretel:	And I don't know why our dad didn't say anything. He just said okay and you know left us there.
Therapist:	So your mom was the one who said stay there and your dad didn't speak up? You were hoping he would?
Gretel:	Yeah.
Therapist:	Does that happen a lot?
Gretel:	What?
Therapist:	Your mom says things and makes things happen that don't feel so hot and your dad just does it.
Gretel:	Yeah, he does. He never really says anything. She tells him what to do.
Therapist:	So what happened next?

Gretel: We just followed the stones and we went home. When we got home, um, our mother just said, you know, what took you so long? And get to bed because tomorrow is going to be another early day.

Therapist: Do you think she was happy to see you?

Gretel: Not really.

Therapist: How was that for you?

Gretel: I guess I didn't really want to stay there. I didn't really want to stay there but Hansel said we should.

Therapist: When you're a kid, it's the only place you could go, I guess.

Gretel: Yeah. We don't have any other relatives.

Therapist: So you got back home and even though Mom, doesn't sound like Mom was very nice or happy, it just didn't feel good. You went to bed and then what happened the next day?

Hansel: She woke us up again, kicked the bed. Gave us some more of that stupid bread.

Therapist: That crumby bread, huh.

Hansel: Yeah. She said we were gonna go again.

Gretel: I didn't want to go.

Therapist: You really didn't want to go.

Gretel: No cuz…cuz I knew what was gonna happen.

Hansel: Yeah, I don't know. I, I don't know why we went. But, I didn't take stones this time. I don't know why I didn't take stones either. I guess I thought, well, we had the bread. It didn't taste very good anyway so this time we made a…we made a trail with the bread.

Therapist: Sounds like you both thought this feels a lot like yesterday which doesn't feel very good. Gretel, you knew you didn't want to go. Hansel, right now you're looking at me like you don't really know for sure why you went again. Does that feel real confusing?

Hansel: I mean why, why would we do that?

Therapist: Why would we do what?

Hansel: Why would we go again? I don't know why we went again.

Therapist: What could you have done differently? What else would you have done? Would you sleep?

Hansel: Yeah, I guess. I don't know.

Therapist: Think your mom would really let you sleep?

Hansel: (a little angry) No, cuz she wanted to get rid of us.

Therapist: It doesn't sound as if you had much of a choice. So, you go with your parents and it's pretty much the same as the day before. What happened?

Hansel: Same thing. But, uh, I put breadcrumbs on the ground. This time they went even deeper in the woods. We passed by the place we were before. And, I thought we were going to stop there but then our mother said "No, we're gonna keep going." Our father was wa-a-a-y ahead.

Therapist: And Hansel, as you're walking and you're going deeper and deeper into the woods were you doing anything on the way, as the day before you were laying stones?

Hansel: I was dropping the breadcrumbs.

Therapist: I was wondering because you said you might use the bread...

Hansel: Uh huh.

Therapist: Along the way, but this was farther this time.

Hansel: It was farther.

Therapist: Did you have enough bread for the whole path?

Hansel: Yeah, but we didn't have enough to eat then.

Gretel: Yeah, but I wasn't too hungry. My stomach didn't feel too good.

Therapist: So Gretel, your stomach was upset and you didn't feel good?

Gretel: Yeah.

Therapist: So what happens now? What did your parents do?

Gretel: They said "Sit down and eat and they didn't come back again. And this time we fell asleep like before but we didn't wake up until the next day. And they were gone.

Therapist: So you slept all night and Gretel you were originally upset...

Gretel: I didn't cry this time. I was kinda mad.

Therapist: Why were you mad?

Gretel: Because we were stupid.

Therapist: You blamed yourself.

Gretel: We were stupid cuz we went. We knew that was, I knew, I knew that was what was going to happen.

Therapist: So did you think it was your fault?

Gretel: No. I just thought it was stupid that we let them take us out in the woods and leave us.

Therapist: You felt that you should have done something differently, not go and that meant you're stupid or...

Gretel: Yeah but we had to go. We didn't have any choice either. I just shouldn't have fallen asleep maybe.

Therapist: So what's next.

Gretel: Well, his (nods toward Hansel) stupid breadcrumbs didn't work. The birds ate 'em all.

Therapist: Ah, the birds found the bread so you couldn't follow the path. Wow. The two of you realized that? Hansel, you saw that? Gretel, you saw that?

Hansel: Yeah well you know, what was I supposed to do?

The children become obviously angry at each other. Looks are exchanged and some comments are thrown back and forth. The therapist continues to direct them in conversation.

Therapist: You screwed up and…

Hansel: Yeah. Yeah I mean...

Gretel: You know, I don't know why I let HIM take care of me either. I mean that was just, he's so stupid. (To Hansel) Why didn't you take stones this time?

Therapist: You were kind of bugged at each other, like why didn't you do the right thing. Gretel you were feeling like you were kind of stupid and Hansel he didn't take care of me. He brought this stupid bread instead of the stones. So you were kind of irritated with each other, it sounds like.

Gretel: Yeah I mean, he's stupid like my father is stupid, I guess.

Therapist: Hansel, what do you think about that?

Hansel: Well you know, I didn't think I was that stupid. And it seemed like a good idea. And we had the bread and it didn't taste good so why not use it? And the stones were heavy in my pocket (a little angry), so I wanted to take the bread instead.

Therapist: Sounds like you did the best you could. Then what happened?

Hansel: Yeah. And I thought the stones from yesterday were gonna be there too. I don't know where they went. I guess we took a different way in the woods too.

Therapist: Yeah, why wouldn't the stones have been there?

Hansel: We must of taken a different way.

Therapist: A different way?

Hansel: But it's just, you know, and…yeah, she didn't cry this time, but I…I had the idea that we should just try to find our way back home. So we did. We tried to find our way back home. But we didn't make it. And we saw this bird and this bird, it just seemed like a good idea to follow it and it took us to the edge of the woods.

Therapist: You tried to find your way out of the forest?

Hansel: Well, find our way home. Our house is kind of in the forest.

Therapist: But you weren't sure of how to get back?

Hansel: Right.

Therapist: And then for some reason, the bird seemed like it knew kind of where it was going and you decided to follow it?

Hansel: It seemed like a good idea.

Therapist:	Sounds like a pretty good idea. Doesn't sound like you had a lot of other things you could have done at that time?
Hansel:	No, not really.
Therapist:	And Gretel wasn't crying too bad. Gretel sounds like you were still more angry than...
Gretel:	And hungry.
Therapist:	Hungry. It's hard to be hungry in the middle of the woods, huh? (Gretel nods her head) Yeah. You're angry and you're lost, trying to find your way home. And you really want to eat something and…
Gretel:	We came to this, this bridge and there was this house. This house, and this house, well it ended up being the witch's house. But we didn't know it. It was a food house.
Therapist:	A food house?
Gretel:	Yeah, cookies. Gingerbread...
Therapist:	You mean it was made out of food?
Gretel:	I was... Yeah. I was hungry so, I really didn't think and I don't care, I was hungry.
Therapist:	Are you trying to make an excuse as to why you saw the candy and said "Well, it doesn't really matter. I was hungry?
Gretel:	(shrugs shoulders) Yeah, well you know.
Therapist:	You were hungry and it sounds like there was a lot of good food on that house.
Gretel:	Yeah.
Therapist:	Yeah.

Gretel: It was, it was a pretty house and it looked really yummy. And...

Therapist: Tell me more. You said it was pretty. Tell me what was pretty about it.

Gretel: Well, the colors and, you know, candy is pretty and cookies are pretty.

Therapist: (thoughtfully) Oh. So you went and decided to eat at the house?

Gretel: Yep. And putting it in my pockets. Just in case we needed it later.

Therapist: So, you were making plans already to have what you needed to get home?

Gretel: Yeah, I guess.

Therapist: That's pretty smart. I think, Gretel, I think that's pretty smart. What do you think Hansel?

Hansel: Yeah, for a girl.

Therapist: (laughs) For a girl. There you go. I hear ya. You're the big brother, so sounds like you really take the job of being a leader and taking care of her very seriously.

Hansel: Yeah.

Therapist: It's okay that she did that but she's a girl.

Hansel: (nods) Hm hm.

Therapist: Yeah. And were you near the house too?

Hansel: Yeah I, I ate some of it. I guess I put some in my pocket. Not as much as she did though.

Therapist:	Not as much as she did. Well, then what happened?
Hansel:	Then this lady came to the door. She asked who was eating her house.
Gretel:	I said it was the wind.
Hansel:	She didn't believe that so she said it was kids and she opened the door and there we were. She looked really nice and she kind of looked like, I guess, if I knew my grandma, she looked like my grandma. Then we went inside and she gave us nice warm clothes. She had nice furniture and there was a fire in the fireplace.
Therapist:	It was nice and warm in there.
Gretel:	She gave us some soup and told us we could stay there. And then she showed us where we could sleep.
Therapist:	And what were you thinking of this old grandma like lady that helped you get warm and dry and gave you some good food and…
Gretel:	Well, I was thinking that it was better than being in the woods.
Hansel:	Well, you know, I figured it was dark outside and we could sleep here.
Therapist:	It felt like it might be a good place to be instead of out in the cold and the dark? This felt like it was okay, like things were going to be okay...
Hansel:	Yeah and I don't, I don't think I would have minded if it stayed like that.
Therapist:	Hmm. Sounds like she really felt like a nice lady in that moment...

Hansel: Yeah.

Therapist: A real grandma. You said you didn't know your grandma so what was she doing? I know you said she fed you and she was nice, but what were some of the really special things she was doing right then that made you feel that she was like your grandma?

Hansel: Well, the house was warm. She smelled good. The house smelled good too.

Therapist: (laughs) All that good food and it's warm and there's a fire in the fireplace.

Hansel: Um you know, she was really…um…she was really nice.

Therapist: Were you relieved at all to finally be in a warm place?

Hansel: Well, yeah.

Gretel: I was happy not to be out in the dark alone.

Hansel: It was nice to be dry.

Therapist: So then what happened?

Hansel: Then we got sleepy. You know, we were walking a lot that day. We got sleepy and she showed us where we could sleep and I don't remember until the next morning. But, the next morning...

Gretel: I thought we were back home. Somebody was kicking the bed and telling us to get up.

Therapist: You thought maybe it was your mother?

Gretel: Yeah but it was that old woman.

Therapist: She was really different then.

Gretel:	Yeah. She was psycho. (Laughs a little)
Therapist:	(laughs too.) That sounds really scary, Gretel.
Gretel:	And you know…she just grabbed us. Yanked us out of bed. She just pulled us. I don't know, I never seen an old lady move like that. She pulled us out into the yard and threw him into a cage. Locked the door.
Therapist:	Hansel, she threw you into a cage?
Hansel:	(looking down) Yeah.
Therapist:	Scary things were happening really quick. You were fed and dry and …
Hansel:	I could have taken her.
Therapist:	You could have taken her?
Hansel:	I guess I was just surprised.
Therapist:	She had been what, so nice the night before?
Hansel:	Yeah.
Therapist:	Were you pretty surprised?
Hansel:	Yeah. I mean, I called her a bitch and she told me to shutup, she said "Or I killed you now."
Therapist:	She threatened to kill you?
Hansel:	Yeah.
Gretel:	Then she made me work. She made me work all around her house.
Therapist:	What did she make you do for her?
Gretel:	Clean. Cook. Feed my brother.

Therapist: And Hansel, what were you doing then?

Hansel: Sitting in a cage.

Therapist: What was that like?

Hansel: Well, I couldn't get out. Couldn't uh…go anywhere. I was hungry until Gretel fed me. And, it was boring. But it was, you know, kind of scary too.

Therapist: You were in the cage, so you were watching Gretel clean and do other things she was told. What was that like for you?

Hansel: I don't know. I just, uh...Gretel didn't cry.

Therapist: She didn't cry? Gretel, it seems like when we first started talking a lot of this story *?

Gretel: Well, I was working on thinking about what I could do. I know, um, you know Hansel, he always takes care of me and he couldn't do anything. He was in a cage.

Therapist: So you were thinking. What kinds of things were you thinking you could do?

Gretel: I thought whether I could kill that old witch. I thought whether I could maybe steal the key and let my brother out in the middle of the night but that didn't work.

Therapist: So you were really thinking, how in the middle of the night you could get up and get away and what can I do to help my brother? How can we keep this old lady from finding us?

Gretel: Yeah. Um, cuz, you know, I uh, she didn't lock me up like she locked him up. She just always watched me so I couldn't… couldn't leave and I wouldn't leave Hansel anyway. I mean, I guess I could have gone for help. I don't know where I would have got help. I don't know what would have happened to Hansel while I was gone, so I figured I better stay.

Therapist: You decided to stay?

Gretel: Yeah, and I thought I should just do what the old witch told me to do too, so she didn't…didn't hurt us.

Therapist: Just gotta get through it?

Gretel: (nods) Uh huh.

Therapist: So what happened...you were thinking about "Can I get away? Can I get some help from somewhere? Get away from this lady. Get away from our parents. *? I'll just keep doing what she says and...

Gretel: Well, every day she would go and tell Hansel to stick his finger out of the cage. Then she would test him to see if he was fat enough to eat.

Therapist: She was feeding him a lot to get him fat?

Gretel: Uh huh, but you know, he was smart.

Hansel: Yeah (laughing), I kept a chicken bone and I just stuck out the chicken bone instead of my finger so she thought I wasn't fat enough and she wouldn't eat me. But then one day she decided she didn't want to wait anymore. She was gonna to eat me anyway.

Therapist: Hansel, that was really smart.

Hansel: Yeah well (shrugs) I guess *?

Therapist: Then what happened?

Gretel: (Somewhat matter of fact) So, she told me to start the fire in the oven so she could cook (pauses) Hansel. And then...

Therapist: What were you thinking when she said that?

Gretel: I wasn't gonna (pauses) cook my brother. So, I told her I didn't know how, I didn't know how to make the oven hot. Cuz, I wasn't gonna do it.

Therapist: So you lied to her.

Gretel: Yeah, hmm. So she said she would show me how. And when she showed me how I kicked her in the oven and we burned her up.

Therapist: Wow, you felt better. You saw a moment when you could do something?

Gretel: Yeah, I was waiting.

Therapist: Always waiting. Always watching.

Gretel: And um, I got the key and let my brother out. And um, that old witch screamed.

Therapist: When she was cooking.

Gretel: Smelled bad but I didn't care.

Therapist: Stinky huh?

Gretel: (nods)

Therapist: Yeah. And Hansel, what did it feel like when you got out of the cage?

Hansel: Well, it felt really good. My legs hurt. I was sitting most of the time in the cage.

Therapist: You were scrunched up.

Hansel: Yeah.

Therapist: For a long time?

Hansel: Yeah. And uh, we still didn't know where to go but I...

Gretel: Hansel thought maybe there would be something in the old witch's house. And uh, you know, I don't believe in stealing things, but the old witch was dead and I don't care. She tried to kill us and um, we found a whole bunch of good stuff in her house and we took it.

Therapist: So you took what you needed in order to get back. The old witch was dead, the house was still there.

Gretel: Uh huh. Well, what we didn't eat.

Therapist: That you didn't eat.

(Children laugh) (Therapist laughs)

Therapist: Yeah. I hear that.

Gretel: So we took her stuff and um, there was some uh…some pearls and some gems. And we filled our pockets with those and…

Hansel: Yeah well, you know, our mother probably would have been happy if we gave her that stuff but we weren't gonna give that to her either. So we just went and we walked and we walked and we came to a lake. It was big and we couldn't get over the lake. Couldn't get around the lake. But we knew somehow we had to go across the lake.

Therapist: How did you cross the lake?

Hansel: Um. This swan came and gave us a ride.

Gretel: But it wasn't very big. It was only big enough to take one of us at a time. She wanted to take me across the lake and I told her "No, take my brother and then come back for me." And that's what we did.

Therapist: Gretel, it sounds like you were still taking care of your brother. And Hansel, she was *?

Hansel: Yeah well, you know, maybe she just thought I should test it first (chuckles). (Children laugh)

Therapist: (Laughs) Just in case it didn't stay on top of the water, right? (Still laughing) See if the swan could really get you across. You think that's what it was about?

Hansel: (Thoughtful) Um, not really. She was (pauses) braver than she was at home.

Therapist: She had a lot of practice looking out for you. *?

Hansel: Yeah.

Therapist: So Hansel, the swan, did it get you across okay?

Hansel: It did, yeah. It came back for Gretel and brought her over. Then, um, we just kept walking and somehow we found our way home.

Therapist: You still had the pearls and the gems?

Hansel: Uh huh.

Therapist: You're gonna keep them for yourselves, it sounds like.

Hansel: Uh huh.

Therapist: And then you got home, were your mom and dad there?

Hansel: Yeah, and our father said he was glad to see us. And our mom didn't say anything.

Gretel:	But, we really didn't care.
Therapist:	Why would you care what your mom said, it sounds like before?
Gretel:	Well, it would be nice to have a real mother but , you know, she's not. You know, she's just, she's just gonna, she's the same.
Therapist:	So Hansel and Gretel, you've been home now for how long?
Gretel:	(squirms) A month.
Therapist:	Is there (changes her question). So, you told me a really big story. A lot of things happened. Is there anything else in the story you wanted to tell me or you think I should know? *?
Gretel:	Uh, I don't know. I think we told you everything.
Therapist:	(nods)
Gretel:	Uh, you know, sometimes I have bad dreams.
Therapist:	That's what I was wondering. You've been back for a month and you just had this really big journey. You said you have bad dreams? That's what I was going to ask, how you've been feeling? Maybe, Gretel, you could tell me what's been happening since you've been home. Gretel, you've had some really bad dreams?
Gretel:	Um, some bad dreams. I don't tell anybody though cuz, I tell Hansel, he listens but I'm not gonna tell them anything.
Therapist:	Anything else? Have either of you been having any trouble eating or?
Gretel:	(thoughtful) Mm, uh, not really.
Therapist:	Are you eating more or less?

Gretel: Maybe a little more.

Therapist: You're eating a little more?

Gretel: But there's not always, there's not always enough.

Therapist: Not always enough.

Gretel: Sometimes we just go out in the woods and we get some berries and whatever we need and we just eat it and we don't say anything.

Therapist: Sounds like the two of you have really gotten better at getting what you need on your own. How about you Hansel, have you had any nightmares? Any bad dreams?

Hansel: Not really, but you know, I don't, I kind of, kind of feels funny sometimes, cuz I don't really have anybody to really take care of. You know, she takes care of herself now.

Therapist: That's something that you used to do and you did it really well. Do you miss that?

Hansel: A little, but, you know, I, I guess we're more like equal now. We're the same. So, we just kind of do what we do and...

Therapist: So it's a change...

Hansel: I'm never gonna be like my father. You know, he's stupid and he's weak. I'll never be like my father.

Therapist: Sounds like you feel really strongly about that. That's really important to you, not to be like your father.

Hansel: Yeah.

Therapist: DO you feel that more now, since you got back?

Hansel:	Um, I feel, I don't feel as strong as I used to feel maybe, but I'm never, I'm not as weak as he is. I'm never gonna be that weak.
Therapist:	So sometimes... Sounds like you've got a couple of things going on there, Hansel. Sometimes you feel not as strong as maybe you did before when you were your sister's protector. You knew what your job was in the family. But then, also sometimes you think about, it's really important not to be weak like your dad.
Hansel:	Yep.
Therapist:	Like that's maybe a little more important to you now than maybe before.
Hansel:	But I wouldn't be like my mother either. She just pushes him around. I'm not gonna push Gretel around.
Gretel:	You won't cuz I won't let you.
Therapist:	(laughs)
Children	(laugh)
Therapist:	Gretel, you're good at taking care of yourself now, right? You're not going to let anyone push you around, sounds like.
Gretel:	Well, sometimes he tries to take care of me. That's okay.
Therapist:	You let him a little bit.
Gretel:	Yeah, but I don't, I don't ne-e-ed it...
Therapist:	(nods)
Gretel:	as much.

Therapist: (nods) Anything else going on? I mean, are you all, are you all back in school now? Do you see any other kids in the forest or anything? Or, do you have any friends?

Hansel: Well, we never really did. Um, we were home schooled.

Therapist: Yeah, so your mom and dad kept you close to home.

Hansel: Yeah. You know, but that's okay cuz you know, I'm, I'm gonna be sixteen next year. And then...

Therapist: You're gonna be a young man.

Hansel: Then probably I'll, I'll get a job or something. It won't be too long I'll be able to buy a house and um, Gretel I will go and live someplace else.

Therapist: Sounds like you have the hope that you can go and do something.

Hansel: (adamantly) I'm not staying here.

Therapist: You told me a really important story about something that happened to the two of you and you shared with me that it was frightening and you got angry and a whole lot of really tough things happened. And, then you got through it. You had to do a lot of things to get through it and you did. You got home. Things are still not really good at home and um, you feel differently because of what happened. You know, like before Gretel, your brother was the big protector and you were the little sister. Now you're much stronger and you don't need as much taking care of. And Hansel, sometimes you don't really know what to do with that because it's like you don't have your job anymore. Um, I asked if you—here, here I asked if you guys were having any problems. Gretel, you were having some nightmares. I'm wondering how, how could I help you? Like if you came back and we took some time together and talk more about what happened how do you think it might help?

Gretel:	(thoughtfully) Mm, I don't know.
Therapist:	How would you like to feel differently than you do now? What would you want to change?
Gretel:	Well I guess, I guess that killing the old witch doesn't bother me too much because I had to do it, but you know, when I have bad dreams that's really what I'm dreaming about.

After Gretel explained a little about her nightmares, the therapist set an appointment to meet with each child separately. This initial interview took approximately one hour, the time a typical counseling session might last.

Not only do we gain insight into the aftermath of this hero-journey story, but we find new meaning in the plot and actions taken by the characters. This is an interesting and valuable means for exploring stories from a new perspective.

Bibliography

Bettleheim, B. *The Uses of Enchantment.* New York: Random House. 1976.

Courlander, Harold. "Two Friends: How They Parted." *The King's Drum.* New York: Harcourt, Brace, & World, Inc. 1962.

Cox, Allison & Albert, David H. *The Healing Heart: Families.* Canada: New Society Publishers. 2003. ISBN 0-86571-466-5.

Cox, Allison & Albert, David H. *The Healing Heart: Communities.* Canada: New Society Publishers. 2003. ISBN 0-86571-468-1.

Elder, John & Wong, Hertha D. *Family of Earth & Sky.* Boston: Beacon Press. 1994. ISBN 0-8070-8529-4.

Estes, Clarissa Pinkola. *Women Who Run with the Wolves.* New York: Ballantine. 1995. ISBN 0-345-39681-2.

Fincher, Suzanne F. *Coloring Mandalas.* Boston: Shambhala. 2000. ISBN 1-57062-563-2. Riordan, James. *The Woman in the Moon.* New York: Dial Books for Young Readers. 1962. ISBN 0-8037-0194-2.

Fisher, R., Ury, W.L. & Patton, B. *Getting to Yes.* Penguin Group. 1981.

Forest, Heather. *Wisdom Tales From Around the World.* Little Rock: August House. 1996.

Fontana, D. *The Secret Language of Symbols.* San Francisco: Cronicle Books. 1993.

Herman, Judith. *Trauma and Recovery.* Perseus Books. 1992.

Hamilton & Weiss. *Children Tell Stories: Teaching and Using Storytelling in the Classroom.* Katonah, New York: Richard C. Owen Publishers. 2005.

Holt, D. & Mooney, B. *Ready-To-Tell Tales*. Little Rock: August House. 1994.

MacDonald, Margaret Read. *Peace Tales*. New Haven: Linnet Books. 1992.

Martin, Rafe. *Rough Face Girl*. Paper Star. 1998.

Mooney, B. & Holt,D. *The Storyteller's Guide*. August House.1996.

Nic Leods, Sorche. "The Weeping Lass at the Dancing Place." *Twelve Black Cats*.

Simms, Laura. *Making Peace*. Chicago: Earwig Recordings.

Simms, Laura. *Women and Wild Animals*. http://www.amazon.com/Women-Wild-Animals-Morning-Welcome/dp/ 0939643375.

Simms, Laura. "Boy Who Hid in the King's Heart." Parabola Magazine: Issue on SOUL.

Yolan, Jane. *Favorite Folktales from Around the World*. New York: Pantheon Books. 1986.

Wolkstein, Diane. *The Magic Orange Tree*. New York: Schocken Books. 1997. ISBN 0-8052-1077-6.

Video:

Masks from Many Cultures. Crystal Video. 1-800-255-8629, ISBN 1-56290-085-4.

Index

Q

R

S

About the Author

Lorna MacDonald Czarnota is an award-winning storyteller and author who has delighted audiences in schools, libraries, festivals and conferences throughout the United States, Canada, and Ireland with traditional and original stories since 1985. Her work features historical presentations, storytelling, writing workshops, and motivational presentations. She specializes in work with at-risk youth, Celtic folklore, and the use of music and song to enhance story. She is the author of *Medieval Tales that Kids Can Read and Tell, Legends, Lore and Secrets of Western New York, Wicked Niagara: the Sinister Side of the Niagara Frontier, Breadline Blue, American and Pioneer Sites of Upstate New York: Westward Trails From Albany to Buffalo* and has stories in other anthologies and magazines.

Lorna holds a Bachelor in Creative Studies for Young Children, a Masters in Special Education, and certification in Trauma Counseling. She is the founder and executive director of Crossroads Story Center, Inc., a not-for-profit for reaching at-risk youth through story.

Lorna began working with at-risk youth in 1994, and continues to run programs in run-away shelters, group homes, treatment centers and other venues. She is a leader in this work within the national and international storytelling community. She has presented at storytelling conferences and festivals throughout the United States. Lorna has also worked with teachers and parents of at-risk youth. In 2004, Lorna presented her work to storytellers in Ireland and worked there with inner-city youth. Her work with at-risk youth has expanded to storytelling with abused women and their children, and communities in disaster. Educators of young children in Blacksburg Virginia, brought Lorna to work with the community at large in April 2007, following the shooting on the Virginia Tech campus. Recognized by her community Lorna is the recipient of the 2006 Oracle Award from the National Storytelling Network, the Hopevale Incorporated Volunteer of the Year Award, Storytelling World Award, and was nominated as a Univera, United Way Community Hero.

www.crossroadsstorycenter.com
www.lornamacdonaldczarnota.com
www.storyhavenstudio.com